# The Breakfast Club

we built this city **on**

# BACON ROLLS

# The Breakfast Club

Jonathan Arana-Morton

## Glorious Rise & Shine Recipes

EBURY PRESS

# THE BREAKFAST CLUB

## Eggs

The Perfect Eggs 13
Poached 13
Fried 13
Scrambled 13
Posh Eggs on Toast 16
Steak & Eggs 17
Huevos Rancheros 18
Bean Shakshuka 20
Turkish Eggs 23
Eggs Benedict 24
Grand Royale 26
Eggs Al Benny 28
Club Med Benedict 29
Pulled Pork Beer Cheese Benedict 30
Ham, Egg & Chips Benedict 32
Nashville Fried Chicken 34
Steak & Truffle Benedict 35

## Pancakes

Classic Pancakes 39
Pancakes & Bacon 39
Pancakes, Cream & Berries 41
The All American 42
Ham So Eggcited 43
The Big Stack 44
Lemon Meringue Pancakes 46
Mississippi Mud Pie Pancakes 47
The Chocolate & Bacon Bananaganza 49
Cherry Pie Pancakes 50
Blueberry Cheesecake Pancakes 51

## Cafness

The Greasy Spoon 57
Rise & Shine 57
The Full Monty 59
Veggie Spoon 61
Salt Beef Bubble & Squeak 62
Sweet Potato, Savoy Cabbage Bubble & Squeak 63
The Perfect Bacon Roll 64
Bacon, Avo & Applewood Sandwich 56
Posh Sausage Sandwich 67
The Breakfast Club Burger 70
Avo, Egg & Cheese 71
Chorizo & Cheddar Sausage Rolls 73
Chicken Kiev Sandwich 74

## The Great American Diner

Grilled Cheese 79
Disco Fries 80
Homemade Hash Browns 82
Breakfast Burrito 83
Cornflake Crusted Fire Wings 84
Fried Chicken Escalopes 85
Buttermilk Fried Chicken 86
Jonnie's Mac & Cheese 89
The Breakfast Club Club 90
Reuben Sandwich 93
Philly Cheese Patty Melt 94
Pulled Pork Sandwich 96
Salt Beef Hash 97
Crunchy Nut French Toast 99
Classic French Toast 99
Passion fruit Cheesecake Waffle 100

## Rise & Shine

Pineapple & Lime Overnight Oats 105
Blueberry Overnight Oats 105
Maple Porridge 105
Banana Bread 108
Banana Bread with Roasted Peaches 109
Breakfast Sundae 110
Guilt-Free Banana Split 113
Smashed Avo & Pico de Gallo Toast 115

## Batch & Sauce

Vegan Chorizo 119
Scrambled Tofu 119
The Breakfast Club Beans 120
Salt Beef 120
Beer Pulled Pork 121
Cheese Sauce 122
Beer Cheese 122
Fried Green Tomatoes 123
Homestyle Potatoes 124
Caramelised Onions 126
Pink Pickled Onions 126
Pickled Red Cabbage 126
Burnt Onion Cream 126
Mojo Picón 127
Chimichurri 127
Pico de Gallo 127
Virgin Mary Mayo 128
Reuben Sauce 128
Chipotle & Harissa Mayo 128
Herb Aioli 128
Chipotle & Tomato Sauce 129
Hollandaise 130
Dill Pickles 131
Wing Sauce 131
Cherry Cream 132
Blueberry Cream 132
Vanilla Cream 132
Lemon Cream 132
Passion Fruit Cheesecake Cream 134
Vanilla French Toast Mix 134
Chocolate Cream 134
Cheesecake Cream 134
Cherry Compote 135
Blueberry Compote 135
Salted Caramel & Chocolate Sauce 135

## Drinks

Blood Mary Batch Mix 139
The Breakfast Club Bloody Mary 139
Ruby Murray Mary 140
Greek Bloody Mary 140
Rise & Shine Mimosa 143
Marmalade Margarita 143
Breakfast Mai Tai 143
Breakfast Negroni 144
Morning Mojito 144
Rumble in the Jungle 147
Pink Responsibly 147
Jalisco Sunset 148
Limoncello & Basil Spritz 148
Watermelon Daiquiri 149
Elvis Milkshake 149
Pink Maple Lemonade 149
The Big Breakfast Smoothie 151
Morning Glory 151
Blue Monday Smoothie 152
Green is Good Smoothie 152

## Extras

Acknowledgements 154
Index 155

# SOHO, LONDON.
### Some day in September 2005. Early.

Really Early. Life always starts early at The Breakfast Club.

A mad dash down Dean Street, right on Carlisle, dodging the oncoming traffic and through to Wardour before finally arriving at a bright egg yolk yellow-fronted caf on D'Arblay Street. But this was not your everyday, late for work, mad dash. This one involved a shopping trolley full of bacon, sausages, eggs and cheese. A supermarket sweep's worth of breakfast goods careering through the streets of Soho, pushed by a very flustered, red-faced man (me) in an apron.

It wasn't the first time I'd forgotten to call in the next day's deliveries and it wouldn't be the last. It would become a ritual I'd repeat many times over the first few months of The Breakfast Club. 20 years later, despite the chaos of those first few months, here I am writing our first book. We've opened 17 cafs in that time and that first one is still there, a couple of streets down from Oxford Street, slap bang in the centre of one of the world's great cities.

The chaos? Well, that's still there. I may not be running through Soho with a supermarket trolley anymore, but the everyday of running restaurants throws up its own unique challenges. One simple day in hospitality, a good friend of mine once told me, is the impossible dream. I think he's right.

The Breakfast Club is a product of more than 40 years of friendship. Me (Jonathan) and my best friend and now sister-in-law, Ali, met when we were 12 in a West Yorkshire village in the mid 80s. *Think Stranger Things* without the strange things, Yorkshire Things. All the kids on BMX bikes and synth-pop soundtracks, but not a lot happening. A lovely existence in a lovely setting.

Since then our lives have been inextricably linked through friendship, family and The Breakfast Club. She is now aunt to my three kids, while I'm uncle to her and my brother's three. Wonderful symmetry.

Some of you may remember *Cheers*, the 80s sitcom set in a Boston bar. It used to air every Friday night, 9pm, Channel 4. We're talking a time before Netflix, before *Friends*, a time when there were only four channels on TV. As teenagers, Ali and I binged on endless VHS tapes of recorded episodes. It was here that we first decided what we were going to do when we were 'grown ups'.

'We'll open a bar!'

To us, a caf was our Yorkshire twist on a Boston bar. Certainly, if Cheers didn't exist neither would The Breakfast Club. You'd be sat here reading someone else's book.

### Everyone is WELCOME

Introduction  6

**August 22nd 2005, 2:26pm.**

# OPENING DAY.

The Breakfast Club opened its doors just after lunch. Some might say missing breakfast was a strange decision. We must have tried to open that door four or five times that day, only to make excuses as to why we weren't ready. The moment you open your restaurant for the first time is both the most nerve-wracking moment of your life and also, surprisingly, underwhelming.

You turn the closed sign round to 'open' and wait. Wait ten minutes. Nobody. Wait half an hour. Nobody. Then they walk in. Customer number one. The relief. The joy. The rest is history. Between you and me, customer number one was a friend called James. His £13 that day made up half our takings.

The plan – well, kind of plan – was home-cooked food in a place we'd want to take our friends. A place 'where everybody knows your name'. Ali brought her Yorkshire charm to the coffee counter and I tried to cook in the kitchen.

The original Soho caf was a nostalgic nod to Ali's and my childhood. Short on inspiration for decoration we decided to head home to Halifax and collected the contents of our childhood bedrooms – old toys, photographs and Kylie Minogue vinyls. We wanted people to be reminded of home.

And it seemed to work. The one thing that took us by surprise was how welcoming and, at times, forgiving our customers were at the start. We got a real sense that people were willing us to succeed. That people came back was, in no small part, down to Ali, whose warmth every morning made everyone feel at home. So while I may have taken too long to get them their food, they still returned. To the early adopters or the millions of people who have visited and had breakfast with us over the years: thank you for giving us a chance.

# WE BUILT THIS CITY ON BACON ROLLS.

A bacon sandwich is where it all started for us. So simple but so easy to get wrong. I know our kitchens are in a good place when the bacon rolls are just right. I always wanted to be that person who opened a place with two menu items – great bacon rolls and fabulous coffee. Nothing else. But I was never brave enough. This would be a very short book if that was the case. Chapter 1 – Bacon Rolls. The End. In the early 2000s Ali and I both found ourselves living next to Chapel Market in Angel, north London. It was, at the time, a veritable Mecca for the great British caf. Every second shopfront seemed to be serving fabulous bacon rolls and classic full English breakfasts. But there was always going to be more to all this than a bacon roll.

At some point in the last two decades, breakfast became an event. The journey we've been on with breakfast and brunch is the journey we took at The Breakfast Club. Consider this, if you'd have mashed an avocado, served it on a slice of toast and called it breakfast in 2005 you'd have raised an eyebrow. If you called it 'smashed', the second eyebrow would have cranked up too.

And don't get me started on the idea that you might then take a photo of your smashed avo toast. It's 2005, that didn't happen. You couldn't tweet about it and you wouldn't post on Instagram about it. You'd just eat it. The world moves fast, our analogue caf grew up in a digital world.

The rest of our food journey was inspired by two unrelated events. The first, in 1989, was my first taste of Eggs Benedict on a trip to Florida with Ali and her family. Breakfasts would never be the same again for that 17 year old from Halifax. Through my 20s the US gained mythical status and I tried to go on holiday there whenever I could. There is no better place to sit than the counter of a diner ordering endless coffee refills with piles of pancakes and bacon so crispy it snapped. There still isn't. It's why, whenever we can, we put a counter in our cafs. The US has been a huge influence on the food we serve at The Breakfast Club.

The second event came in 2007 as we geared up to open our second caf on the beautiful Camden Passage in Angel. It's here that I met a Canadian chef named Sam. He had long, wild hair and a huge beard (before everyone had one), the kind of person you'd meet on a beach while backpacking across South East Asia. An easy going, wonderful, free spirit. This was our sliding doors moment.

With Sam came the pancakes. the Benedicts and the North American influence we'd always wanted but never been able to authentically deliver. But here's the thing with free spirits, they don't tend to hang around for long. He was there one day and gone the next. Sam may have only been with us for a few months, but he will always be the Godfather of The Breakfast Club menu. Thank you, Sam.

Ali and I are aware of how lucky we've been. There have been many Sams along the way who have had a profound impact on The Breakfast Club. A member of the team once pointed out that I wasn't really good at anything apart from surrounding myself with great people. I think that's what you call a back-handed compliment. He was right though. None of this would have happened without the people who made The Breakfast Club what it is today. And none of these recipes either without the wonderful chefs I've had the honour of working with. I'm secretly proud of my one and only talent. It's served me well.

The Breakfast Club is a perfect storm of the great British caf and an American diner. The best of all worlds. We have one rule – simple food, made well with great ingredients. It's comfort food, not complex food. The idea was that if we ever got caught short in the kitchen we could all jump on to help. That bodes well for anyone lacking confidence in the kitchen. Breakfast should be simple, quick and easy to make – you've got the rest of your day to be getting on with!

We didn't invent smashed avo on toast, flat whites or Eggs Benedict. We weren't the first people to put bacon and maple syrup on pancakes. We have never been ahead of the curve, always a few steps behind. But we've always had a love for what we do. We make feel-good food. A smile is always our secret ingredient.

I hope I can convey the absolute joy The Breakfast Club has given me this last 20 years. As much as I want you to cook the food on these pages, I'd like to think that somewhere, someone reading this rolls the dice and opens their own place. It's stressful, it's hectic, it's all consuming, but hospitality is the greatest industry in the world. I love it from the very bottom of my heart.

Every so often I'll stand behind the counter in Soho when it's closed and the team have gone home. I'll pop on a tune ('Give Me One Reason', Tracy Chapman) and repeat the words of Sam Malone in the very last episode of *Cheers*...

# 'BOY, I TELL YOU, I'm the luckiest son of a bitch on earth'

9 Introduction

# EGGS
## all day

I hope I've been clear from page one, I'm no Gordon Ramsay. In fact, I was probably the guy Gordon would have helped out on one of his shows. Those first few months felt like a standing start. Going from a competent home cook to working in a commercial kitchen trying to cook for 30 people was all about survival. Every day, watching the last ticket leave the pass was a small victory. My girlfriend (now wife) took to calling me 'bacon head'. I was a living, walking Frazzle. And I was quite literally frazzled every day.

If you looked at our first menu in 2005 you'd notice we didn't offer one very significant breakfast ingredient. Eggs. Our egg yolk yellow caf called The Breakfast Club was not quite ready for eggs. I was not ready for eggs.

Or so most people thought. We built our confidence one egg at a time. For a select few regulars in the know there were 'secret' eggs. When things were quiet and we had things under control a fried egg was available. Scrambled came next and eventually we took on a poached egg, never easy at the best of times!

20 years on, eggs now dominate our menu and rightly so. A super food for some super dishes. Eggs Benedict, Eggs Royale, Eggs on Toast, Huevos Rancheros, eggs this, eggs that. Two decades of making eggs poached, fried or scrambled have taught us a few simple lessons that we'll share with you over the next few pages. Most of all, like we always say – keep it simple.

Gordon did actually visit our caf in Battersea over the years, not as a ranting TV chef, but as a customer with his family. He was always truly lovely with our kitchen team and those chefs still talk about the day Gordon Ramsey came into their kitchen. It's incredible what a lasting impact a few well-chosen, kind words can have. Thanks, Gordon, you made their day.

Serves 1

# THE PERFECT EGGS

## Poached

2 tsp white wine vinegar
2 eggs (as fresh as possible!)

Fill a saucepan with water and add the vinegar. Bring the water to the boil, then reduce to a gentle simmer.

Crack an egg into a small mug, cup or ramekin.

Carefully drop the egg into the middle of the boiling water. Repeat as above with the 2nd egg. Set a timer for 3 minutes.

Carefully remove each egg with a slotted spoon and drain briefly on kitchen paper.

## Fried

4 tbsp vegetable oil
2 eggs (as fresh as possible!)

Put a small frying pan over a medium–high heat and add the oil. After a minute or two, crack the eggs into the pan.

Cook for 3 minutes, carefully spooning some of the oil over the whites of the eggs to ensure the white is evenly cooked and to maintain a runny yolk. Once the white is cooked, use a spatula to carefully remove each egg and drain briefly on kitchen paper.

## Scrambled

2 eggs (as fresh as possible!)
Knob of butter

Crack the eggs into a bowl and use a whisk to break up and combine them until they are smooth and mixed.

Put a non-stick frying pan over a low heat and add the butter. Once the butter is foaming, pour the beaten eggs into the pan. Gently stir and fold with a spatula continuously until the eggs are soft and fluffy.

**Eggs**

# Posh Eggs on Toast

**Weekend eggs with some razzle dazzle**

2 eggs
Knob of butter
1 tsp truffle purée
1 spring onion, finely sliced
50g Parmesan cheese, finely grated
Salt and black pepper, to taste
1 slice sourdough, toasted and buttered

Crack the eggs into a bowl and use a whisk to break up and combine them until they are smooth and mixed.

Put a non-stick frying pan over a low heat and then add the butter. Once the butter is foaming, pour the eggs into the pan. Gently stir and fold with a spatula continuously until the eggs are soft and fluffy.

Fold through the truffle purée, sliced spring onion and half the Parmesan and then season with salt and black pepper.

Put the buttered toast onto a plate and top with the scrambled eggs, then scatter over the remaining Parmesan.

# Steak & Eggs

**The perfect payday breakfast. Treat yourself**

Put the rib-eye steak into a bowl and spoon in the chimichurri. Cover and marinate in the fridge for at least a few hours but preferably overnight. In the restaurant we marinate them for 24 hours.

Remove the steak from the fridge 20 minutes before cooking. When ready to cook, heat a drizzle of oil in a non-stick frying pan over a high heat. Scrape a little of the marinade off the steak and put it into the pan. Cook for 2 minutes on one side, then flip and cook for a further 1 minute on the other side. Remove from the pan and rest on a plate for 3 minutes and then cut it into 1cm thick slices at a 45-degree angle.

Put the buttered toast onto a plate and lay on the steak slices. Top with the fried eggs and then spoon over plenty of the chimichurri to serve.

170g rib-eye steak
4 tbsp Chimichurri (page 127), plus extra to serve
Drizzle of olive oil
1 slice sourdough, toasted and buttered
2 fried eggs (see page 13)

Serves 2

# Huevos Rancheros

**Not just for Mexican farmers**

2 tsp olive oil
4 cooking chorizo
2 tortilla wraps
4 slices red Leicester cheese
6 tbsp Chipotle & Tomato Sauce (page 129), warmed
1 avocado, peeled, destoned and roughly crushed
2 tbsp soured cream
4 fried eggs (see page 13)
4 tbsp Pico de Gallo (use shop bought or see page 127)
4 tbsp canned black beans, drained and warmed
Coriander leaves
½ jalapeño chilli, sliced

Heat the olive oil in a small frying pan over a medium–high heat. Add the chorizo and cook for 4–5 minutes, tossing occasionally, until golden. Remove from the pan and slice when ready to serve.

Heat the grill to medium–high. Put the tortilla wraps on a large baking tray and put the 2 cheese slices next to each other on one half of each tortilla. Fold the tortillas in half over the cheese to create 2 semi-circles. Cook under the grill for 45 seconds–1 minute until the tortillas are golden and the cheese has melted.

Cut the tortillas in half and arrange in a leaf shape on the plates. Spoon on the chipotle and tomato sauce, then the crushed avocado and soured cream and top with the fried eggs. Scatter over the pico de gallo, drained beans, coriander and jalapeño slices, then add the sliced chorizo on the side.

Serves 1

# Bean Shakshuka

**Nothing beats the glorious golden pop of a perfect poached egg**

200g The Breakfast Club Beans (page 120)
1 roasted pepper from a jar, drained and sliced into 1cm strips
1 avocado, peeled, destoned and crushed
Juice of ½ lime
Salt and pepper, to taste
1 thick slice sourdough, toasted
Pinch dried chilli flakes
2 poached eggs (see page 13)
A handful coriander leaves, roughly chopped

Heat a small frying pan over a medium–high heat and scrape in the beans and pepper strips. Stir really well and cook gently until warmed through. Add a splash of water if it looks a little thick.

Mix the avocado with the lime juice and some seasoning, then spread over the toast. Sprinkle with some of the chilli flakes.

Spoon the beans onto the plate and top with the 2 poached eggs. Finish with a sprinkle of coriander.

**Serves 1**

# Turkish Eggs

**Whipped up by Chef Anvar from our Spitalfields caf**

Start by making the burnt chilli butter. Add all of the ingredients to a small saucepan over a medium heat. Stir as the butter melts, then once it is foaming, allow it to cook for 1 minute and then remove it from the heat. Set it aside.

Spoon the Greek yogurt into a bowl and finely grate in the garlic. Season with salt and pepper and squeeze in the lemon juice. Mix well.

Tip the plain flour onto a plate and season well. Coat each of the slices of aubergine in the flour, patting to evenly coat them.

Pour the oil into a frying pan that will snuggly fit the 4 aubergine slices and put the pan over a medium–high heat. Once the oil is shimmering, carefully add the aubergine slices and fry for 2 minutes on each side until they are golden and cooked through.

Spread the garlic yogurt over the bottom of a plate, then top with the aubergine slices and poached eggs. Briefly warm up the burnt butter, then spoon it all over. Scatter with the coriander leaves, sliced spring onion and shredded mint and serve with the sourdough toast.

125g Greek yogurt
1 small garlic clove, peeled
Salt and pepper, to taste
Juice of ¼ lemon
2 tbsp plain flour
½ aubergine, cut into 4 slices lengthways
6 tbsp vegetable oil
2 poached eggs (see page 13)
1 sliced spring onion
A handful coriander leaves
A few mint leaves, finely shredded
1 large slice sourdough, toast

**BURNT CHILLI BUTTER**
50g butter
1 tsp dried chilli flakes
1½ tsp paprika
1 tsp dried mint

Serves 1

# Eggs Benedict

**The classic. We hear Benedict Cumberbatch is a fan**

4 rashers streaky bacon
1 English muffin, halved horizontally and toasted
2 poached eggs (see page 13)
6 tbsp hollandaise (use shop bought or see page 130), warmed
Black pepper, to serve
A handful chives, finely chopped, to serve

Preheat the oven to 200°C/180°C fan.

Put the bacon rashers on a baking tray and put another baking tray directly on top, to keep the rashers flat. Cook in the oven for 15–20 minutes until the bacon is crisp and golden.

Put the toasted muffin halves on a plate, cut side up. Lay on the crispy bacon slices, top with a poached egg and spoon the warm hollandaise over each. Give each a good crack of black pepper and sprinkle with finely chopped chives to serve.

# Grand Royale

**A breakfast fit for a king, queen or just you on a Saturday**

Serves 1

2 tsp capers, drained and finely chopped
4 cornichons, drained and finely chopped
4 pickled silverskin onions, drained and finely chopped
A small handful dill, finely chopped
6 tbsp hollandaise (use shop bought or see page 130), warmed
1 English muffin, halved horizontally and toasted
A handful rocket leaves
70g cold smoked salmon slices
2 poached eggs (see page 13)
Black pepper, to taste
A handful chives, finely chopped, to serve

Scrape the chopped capers, cornichons, pickled onions and dill into your warm hollandaise and mix well. Keep warm.

Put the muffin halves onto a plate, cut side up. Lay half the rocket on each muffin half, then top with the smoked salmon and a poached egg on each, and then spoon over the warm tartar hollandaise. Finish with a crack of black pepper and a sprinkle of chopped chives to serve.

Serves 1

# Eggs A1 Benny

**Spicy but nicey**

2 cooking chorizo
½ red pepper, deseeded and cut in half lengthways
1 tbsp olive oil for drizzling
1 English muffin, halved horizontally
2 poached eggs (see page 13)
6 tbsp hollandaise (use shop bought or see page 130), warmed
Big pinch paprika

**TO SERVE (OPTIONAL)**
Sliced chilli
Pea shoots

Heat a griddle pan over a medium–high heat

Split the chorizo sausages down the middle, but not all the way through, opening them up like a butterfly. Drizzle the chorizo and pepper pieces with oil and put them on the griddle pan. Griddle them for 3 minutes on each side until they are charred and the pepper is softening. Remove from the pan.

Toast both halves of the muffin on the hot griddle for about 45 seconds on each side.

Put both halves on your plate, cut side up. Lay a piece of pepper on each, then a chorizo sausage, cut side facing up. Put a poached egg onto each sausage, then spoon the warm hollandaise over each.

Sprinkle with paprika and serve with sliced chilli and pea shoots on top, if you like.

*Serves 1*

# Club Med Benedict

**Welcome to Club Med (not just for the 18-30s)**

Scatter the plain flour on a plate and season with salt and pepper. Coat each of the halloumi slices in the flour, patting them to make it stick.

Heat the oil in a non-stick frying pan over a medium–high heat. Carefully lay the halloumi pieces into the oil and fry for 2 minutes on each side, until golden and crisp. Remove and place on a kitchen paper-lined plate.

Mix the pesto through the warm hollandaise.

Put the muffin halves, cut side up, on a plate and divide the crushed avocado between the two. Top with pieces of the chopped sundried tomatoes, then the halloumi pieces. Place a poached egg on each. Spoon the pesto hollandaise over the eggs. Top with a few chopped chives, if you like.

2 tbsp plain flour
Salt and pepper, to taste
4 x 1cm thick slices of halloumi
2 tbsp olive oil
6 tbsp hollandaise (use shop bought or see page 130), warmed
1 tbsp fresh basil pesto
1 English muffin, halved horizontally and toasted
1 avocado, peeled, destoned and crushed
4 sundried tomatoes, drained and chopped
2 poached eggs (see page 13)
A handful chives, finely chopped (optional)

Serves 1

# Pulled Pork Beer Cheese Benedict

**Get some pork on my fork pronto**

100g Beer Pulled Pork (page 121)
1 English muffin, halved horizontally and toasted
2 poached eggs (see page 13)
6 tbsp Beer Cheese (page 122)

**TO SERVE**
Pickled Red Cabbage (page 126)
Sliced drained gherkins

Heat the pulled pork in a small saucepan over a medium heat until hot.

Put the toasted muffin halves onto a plate, cut side up. Spoon the pulled pork onto each half, then top each with a poached egg. Spoon the beer cheese on top.

Serve with pickled red cabbage and gherkins.

# Ham, Egg & Chips Benedict

**Serves 1**

**Nan's tea-time fave, but make it Benedict**

1 potato, peeled and cut into 2mm thick matchsticks
Vegetable oil, for deep-frying and drizzling
salt, to taste
1 gammon steak, cut in half
A good dash Tabasco
A handful chives, finely chopped, plus extra to serve
6 tbsp hollandaise (use shop bought or see page 130), warmed
1 English muffin, halved horizontally and toasted
2 poached eggs (see page 13)
10g Parmesan cheese, finely grated

Tip the potato matchsticks into a large bowl of cold water and gently move around. Drain, then refill and repeat a couple of times, then drain really well through a sieve.

Lay a clean tea towel on a work surface and tip the potato matchsticks into it. Pat really dry.

Fill a saucepan half full with vegetable oil and put over a medium–high heat. Line a shallow bowl with kitchen paper. Use a digital thermometer to heat the oil to 175°C. Carefully lower the potato matchsticks into the oil and cook for 2–3 minutes until golden brown. Use a slotted spoon to carefully lift the potato matchsticks out of the oil and then drain on the kitchen paper. Season with salt.

Heat a frying pan over a medium–high heat and drizzle the gammon steak with a little oil. Fry for 2 minutes on each side until it is golden and caramelised.

Mix the Tabasco and chopped chives into the warm hollandaise.

Put the toasted muffin halves on a plate, cut side up. Lay a slice of gammon on each, then pile on the fried shoestring potatoes. Top each with a poached egg and then the hollandaise. Grate over plenty of Parmesan cheese and sprinkle over some chives to serve.

33 Eggs

# Nashville Fried Chicken

**Serves 1**

**Surely Dolly's favourite Benedict?**

2 freshly made pieces Buttermilk Fried Chicken (page 86
1 tbsp rose harissa
6 tbsp Cheese Sauce (page 122)
1 English muffin, halved horizontally and toasted
6 slices drained gherkin
2 poached eggs (see page 13)
4 pickled chillies, drained and sliced
A handful chives, finely chopped

**NASHVILLE GLAZE**
3 tbsp melted butter
2 tsp cayenne pepper
1 tbsp caster sugar
Big pinch smoked paprika
Big pinch garlic powder
1 tbsp runny honey
Salt and pepper, to taste

Make the Nashville glaze by tipping everything into a bowl with some salt and pepper and whisk together.

Toss the freshly fried chicken in the Nashville glaze.

Whisk the rose harissa into the cheese sauce.

Put the toasted muffin halves on a plate, and top each with the gherkin slices. Put a piece of chicken on top of a muffin half, then top with a poached egg. Spoon the harissa cheese sauce over both eggs. Top with a few slices of pickled chilli and some chopped chives.

**Serves 1**

# Steak & Truffle Benedict

**Raise the steaks at breakfast time**

Heat a non-stick frying pan over a high heat. Drizzle the steak with vegetable oil and season really well with salt and pepper. Once the pan is very hot, carefully lay the steak into the pan and cook for 1½–2 minutes on each side, depending on how you like your steak cooked. Remove from the pan and rest on a plate for a minute, and then cut it into 1cm thick slices at a 45-degree angle.

Whisk the truffle paste into the warm hollandaise.

Spread the toasted muffin halves with the truffle or salted butter.

Put the muffin halves on a plate, cut side up. Lay half the rocket on each muffin half, then top with the sliced steak. Top each with a poached egg, then spoon the hollandaise over the eggs. Finish with a sprinkle of chopped chives.

115g rib-eye steak
Vegetable oil, for drizzling
Salt and pepper, to taste
1 tsp truffle paste
6 tbsp hollandaise (use shop bought or see page 130), warmed
1 English muffin, halved horizontally and toasted
1 tbsp truffle butter (or use salted butter)
A handful rocket leaves
2 poached eggs (see page 13)
A handful chives, finely chopped

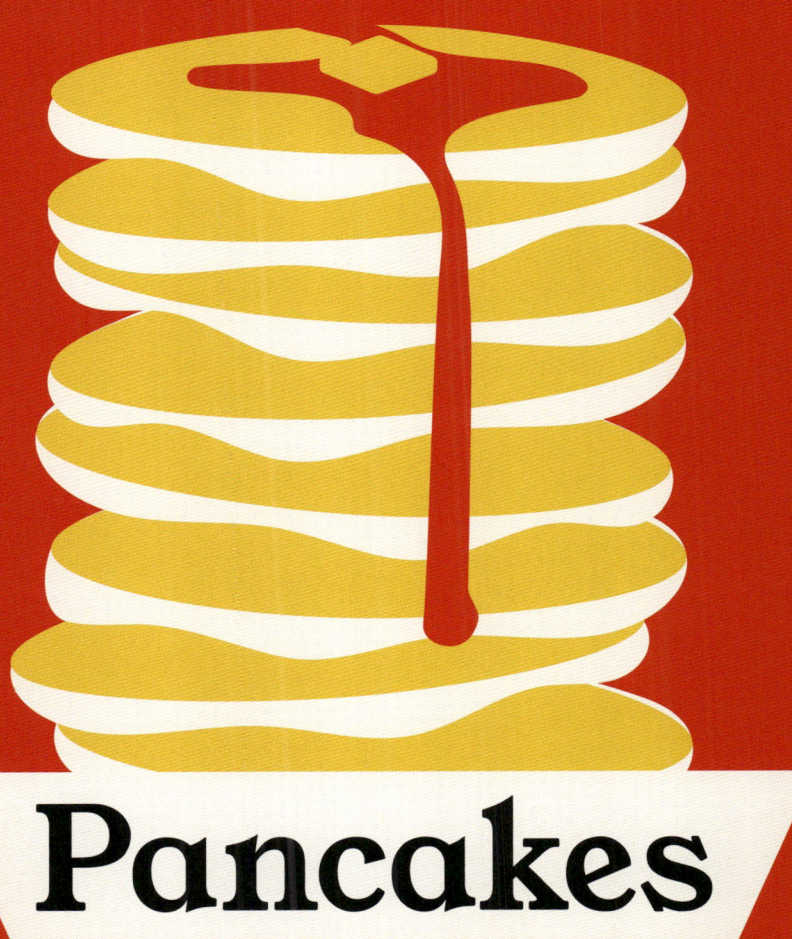

# PANCAKES

I am the proud father of three young children and for an hour every Saturday morning, at breakfast, I am their superhero dad. Pancakes are my superpower. While Mum may be number one parent for the other 167 hours in the week, I 'own' Saturday mornings. I'm pretty sure that if you asked my youngest what my job was she would say: 'Daddy makes pancakes.' Somehow, somewhere along the way, that became my legacy, that's how I'll be remembered. 'Daddy makes pancakes' at home and at work.

At work, for one day a year, The Breakfast Club feels like the centre of the universe. That day falls on what seems to be a random* Tuesday sometime in February or March. Pancake Day. Well actually, it has a host of different names – Mardi Gras, Fat Tuesday, Shrove Tuesday. Pancakes are very much a part of The Breakfast Club story (and mine). Pancake Day is our Christmas, so it feels only right that we dedicate a whole chapter to them.

In any given year our chefs cook up over 1 million pancakes. With some very loose maths, that means The Breakfast Club annual pancake stack is taller than Everest. The tallest we actually build is a 12 stack, which we sell as part of our 12 Pancakes in 12 Minutes Pancake Day Charity Challenge. A mini Everest. Every year I attempt the challenge and rarely make it past basecamp. There are, however, hundreds of people out there who eat this challenge up for breakfast (literally and figuratively). Our current record holder has devoured a 12 stack in 2 minutes and 41 seconds.

So much fuss for such a simple food. There are sweet ones, savoury ones, fat ones, thin ones, healthy ones, American ones, French ones. So many different variations on a theme for something made from three very basic ingredients; milk, flour and eggs.

But pancakes are half the story. A blank canvas. The toppings, now that's where the magic happens. And Pancake Day is our day of magic, the day we really let loose. Many of the dishes you'll find over the next few pages are inspired by some of the many wonderful Pancake Day themes and collaborations we've been a part of over the years.

So here you go. Are you happy to accept superhero status and the crown of king or queen of pancakes in your household? Remember, with great power comes great responsibility. It's a role that's not to be taken lightly.

*We know it's not random. Pancake Day is exactly 47 days before Easter Sunday which lands on the first Sunday after the first full Moon after the spring equinox. Simple!

Serves 1

# Classic Pancakes

350g plain flour
60g caster sugar
2 tbsp baking powder
10g porridge oats
4 eggs
260ml whole milk
50g butter, melted, plus extra for frying
1 tsp vanilla extract

Preheat the oven to 120°C/100°C fan or the lowest temperature.

Mix together the flour, sugar, baking powder and oats in a bowl. In a separate bowl whisk together the eggs, milk, melted butter and vanilla.

Gradually add the wet ingredients to the dry, while whisking, and then continue to whisk until you have a smooth, thick, lump-free batter. Cover and chill in the fridge for 30 minutes.

Heat a large non-stick frying pan over a medium heat and add a knob of butter. Once melted, use a piece of kitchen paper to wipe the butter around the pan.

Add a ladleful of the batter – enough so that the pancake is roughly 12cm in diameter. Repeat, ensuring each pancake has a little space around it, until you have filled the pan.

Leave to cook for 3 minutes, until the tops of the pancakes begin to bubble. Carefully use a spatula to flip them and then cook for a further 2 minutes until they are browned and set.

Remove from the pan and keep warm in the oven while you cook the rest.

# Pancakes & Bacon

3 rashers streaky bacon
3 The Breakfast Club Classic Pancakes: (opposite)
Maple syrup, to serve

Preheat the oven to 200°C/180°C fan.

Put the bacon rashers on a baking tray and put another baking tray directly on top, to keep the rashers flat. Cook in the oven for 15–20 minutes until the bacon is crisp and golden.

Pile the pancakes up on a plate, then top with the crispy bacon. Serve with plenty of maple syrup.

# Pancakes, Cream & Berries

**The OG stack. Thanks Chef Sam**

Lay the 3 pancakes on a plate in a stack. Dust the top pancake with a little icing sugar. Add one of the strawberry quarters to the top (this helps secure the cream). Spoon or quenelle the cream onto the top of the pancakes and then top with the remaining strawberries and the raspberries and blueberries. Pour over the maple syrup to serve.

3 Classic Pancakes (page 39)
Icing sugar, for dusting
4 strawberries, hulled and cut into quarters
75g Vanilla Cream (page 132)
A small handful raspberries
A small handful blueberries
3 tbsp maple syrup, to serve

Serves 1

# The All American

**The dish that made us famous (D-list celebrity famous)**

1 pork sausage
1 tbsp olive oil
4 rashers streaky bacon
100g Homestyle Potatoes (page 124)
2 Classic Pancakes (page 39)
2 fried eggs (see page 13)
Maple syrup, to serve

Preheat the oven to 200°C/180°C fan.

Put the sausage on a baking tray with the oil, toss to coat and then roast for 25 minutes, turning halfway through, until golden and cooked through.

Meanwhile, put the bacon rashers on a baking tray and put another baking tray directly on top, to keep the rashers flat. Cook in the oven for 15–20 minutes until the bacon is crisp and golden.

Scoop the potatoes onto a plate and put the crispy bacon and sausage on too. Add on your pancakes as well as the fried eggs. Serve with maple syrup.

# Ham So Eggcited

**You're eggcited. They're eggcited. Ham eggcited**

Tip the potato matchsticks into a large bowl of cold water and gently move around. Drain, and repeat a couple of times, then drain really well through a sieve.

Lay a clean tea towel on a work surface and tip the potato matchsticks into it. Pat really dry.

Fill a saucepan half full with vegetable oil and put over a medium–high heat. Line a shallow bowl with kitchen paper. Use a digital thermometer to heat the oil to 175°C. Carefully lower the potato matchsticks into the oil and cook for 2–3 minutes until golden brown. Use a slotted spoon to carefully lift the potato matchsticks onto the kitchen paper. Season with salt.

Put the honey mustard glaze ingredients into a small saucepan over a medium heat, bring to the boil and then bubble away for a couple of minutes until combined, glossy and slightly thickened.

Heat a drizzle of oil in a non-stick frying pan over a medium–high heat. Add the ham slices and fry them for 2 minutes, turning halfway through, until lightly golden, then remove them from the pan. Add another drizzle of oil and increase the heat to high. Add the pineapple rings and fry them for 2 minutes on each side until golden.

Put one of the pancakes on a plate and top with half the ham. Drizzle with some of the honey mustard glaze, top with another pancake and the other half of the ham and more honey mustard glaze. Top with the final pancake, the pineapple rings and the fried egg. Add a handful of the shoestring fries on top to serve.

**Serves 1**

1 potato, peeled and cut into 2mm thick matchsticks
Vegetable oil, for deep-frying and drizzling
Salt, to taste
150g sliced ham
2 pineapple rings
3 Classic Pancakes (page 39)
1 fried egg (see page 13)

### HONEY MUSTARD GLAZE
1 tbsp soft brown sugar
2 tsp maple syrup
2 tsp runny honey
1 tsp Dijon mustard

Serves 1

# The Big Stack

**The Godzilla of the pancake world.
Always serving Big Stack energy**

3 rashers streaky bacon
2 hash browns
2 sausages
2 tbsp vegetable oil
3 Classic Pancakes (page 39)
3 tbsp Caramelised Onions (page 126)
4 tbsp Cheese Sauce (page 122 or use shop bought), warmed
1 fried egg (see page 13)
Maple syrup, to serve

Preheat the oven to 200°C/180°C fan.

Put the bacon rashers on a baking tray, put another baking tray directly on top, to keep the rashers flat, and then put the hash browns on the top tray. Roast for 15–20 minutes until the bacon is golden brown and the hash browns are crisp.

Remove the sausages from their skins and tip the meat into a bowl. Use slightly damp hands to form the meat into a 1cm thick patty, slightly wider than the width of your pancakes. Heat the oil in a non-stick frying pan over a medium heat. Add the patty to the pan and cook it for 3 minutes on each side until golden and cooked through.

Remove the patty from the pan. Put the roasted hash browns in the pan, and then press them down with a spatula to squash them into the pan. Cook for 2 minutes on each side until super crisp.

Assembly time. Lay one of the pancakes on a plate and top with the caramelised onions. Add on one of the smashed hash browns, then the sausage patty and a good spoonful of the cheese sauce. Top with a 2nd pancake, a hash brown, the bacon and more of the cheese sauce. Top with a final pancake and the fried egg. Serve with maple syrup to pour over.

Serves 1

# Lemon Meringue Pancakes

**Nan's favourite dessert with a Breakfast Club twist**

3 Classic Pancakes (page 39)
4 tbsp lemon curd
A good spoonful Vanilla Cream (page 132)
1 small meringue nest, crushed

Put one of the pancakes on a plate and top with 1 tablespoon of the lemon curd, then some of the cream and a little of the crushed meringue. Repeat twice more and then finish with a good spoon of the vanilla cream, a drizzle of lemon curd and a final sprinkling of meringue.

Serves 1

# Mississippi Mud Pie Pancakes

One word (a made-up word)...CHOCOLICIOUS

Put the finely chopped dark chocolate in a small heatproof bowl. Pour the cream into a small saucepan and put over a medium heat. Bring to a gentle simmer, then quickly pour over the chocolate. Add a pinch of salt and leave to melt for a minute before stirring until combined. Leave the ganache to cool to room temperature.

Put one of the pancakes on a plate and top with a spoonful of the chocolate ganache and a sprinkling of granola. Repeat this again, then top with a final pancake.

Gently fold the remaining ganache through the vanilla cream so it is rippled. Spoon this onto the pancake stack and sprinkle over the chopped milk and white chocolate pieces, remaining granola and a drizzle of maple syrup.

50g dark chocolate, finely chopped
100ml double cream
Salt
3 Classic Pancakes (page 39)
2 tbsp granola
A good spoonful Vanilla Cream (page 132)
15g milk chocolate, roughly chopped
15g white chocolate, roughly chopped
Maple syrup

Pancakes 48

Serves 1

# The Chocolate & Bacon Bananaganza

**Trust us. This works. Give it a shot**

Preheat the oven to 200°C/180°C fan.

Put the bacon rashers on a baking tray and evenly sprinkle with the soft brown sugar. Put another baking tray directly on top, to keep the rashers flat. Cook in the oven for 15–20 minutes until the bacon is crisp and golden. Roughly chop 3 of the bacon rashers.

Drizzle a non-stick frying pan with the caramel syrup and then add in the banana pieces. Put over a medium–high heat and cook for 1–2 minutes, tossing so the bananas are coated in the caramel sauce but do not soften too much.

Lay one of the pancakes on a plate and top with 2 of the caramelised banana pieces. Drizzle over a third of the salted caramel and chocolate sauce, then add half the chopped bacon.

Lay the next pancake on top and lightly dust with the icing sugar.

Add 2 more banana pieces and the rest of the bacon and half the remaining sauce.

Top with the 3rd pancake, lightly dust with icing sugar and add the remaining banana pieces to the pancake, then spoon or quenelle the vanilla cream on the top. Drizzle with the remaining salted caramel and chocolate sauce, add the remaining bacon rasher to the top and sprinkle with the chopped chocolate.

4 rashers streaky bacon
2 tbsp soft light brown sugar
2 tbsp caramel sauce or syrup
1 banana, peeled and cut lengthways and then cut into 6cm pieces
3 Classic Pancakes (page 39)
60g Salted Caramel & Chocolate Sauce (page 135)
1 tbsp icing sugar
75g Vanilla Cream (page 132)
20g salted caramel chocolate, roughly chopped – we love Tony's!

# Cherry Pie Pancakes

**A cherry nice pancake stack**

75g Vanilla Cream (page 132)
4 tbsp Cherry Compote (page 135)
3 Classic Pancakes (page 39)
2  Lotus Biscoff, crumbled
Maple syrup, to serve

Spoon the vanilla cream into a bowl. Add in 1 tablespoon of the cherry compote and use a spoon to gently fold it through so it looks rippled.

Put one of the perfect pancakes on a plate and top with a spoonful of the cherry compote and a good sprinkle of the crumbled biscuits. Repeat twice more, then finally top with the cherry rippled cream and a final sprinkle of biscuit. Serve with maple syrup for pouring over.

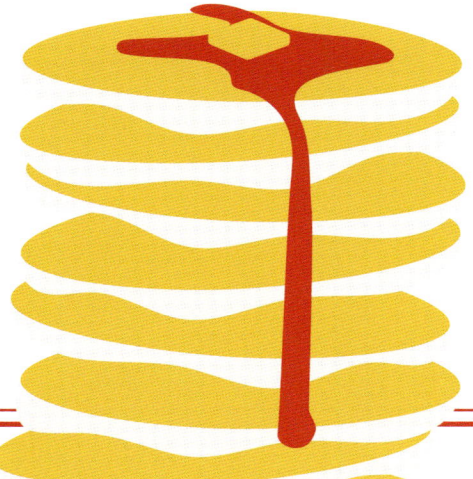

# Blueberry Cheesecake Pancakes

**In the cafs we serve this with a cloud of pink candy floss because why the hell not?!**

Put a pancake on a plate and top with a third of the blueberry compote, then with a third of the cheesecake cream. Repeat this two more times and finish with a handful of candy floss or just a sprinkling of icing sugar, if you like.

3 Classic Pancakes (page 39)
100g Blueberry Compote (page 135), warmed
150g Cheesecake Cream (page 134)
Candy floss or icing sugar, to serve (optional)

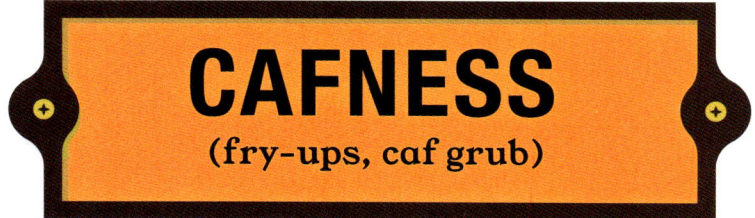

# CAFNESS
## (fry-ups, caf grub)

From one yellow caf to many. It was all quite unexpected and unplanned. All Ali and I ever originally planned or wanted to do was one place. One day we will.

We became known for the queues outside the cafs. We still are. Every so often, even now, a newspaper or critic will be flummoxed by the idea that people would want to queue for The Breakfast Club. One foodie Instagram account, where chefs are asked about the London restaurant scene, has time and again given us the dubious award of…

The most overrated restaurant in London. (I think at the time of writing we are eight-time winners.)

Quite a feat for a caf. But the fact that our yellow caf is even mentioned in the same breath as some of the big budget, big name, all the bells and whistles London restaurants blows our minds. We most definitely take it as a compliment.

What we do is simple. It's made well with a warm, arms wide-open welcome. If after 20 years we still have queues then we're doing something right. Hype normally carries a restaurant through the first couple of years, but not two decades. We don't have a hype team, but we do have a lovely man called Tom who started out front of house in our Hoxton caf, now does all our marketing and got this whole book together.

The reason we believe people still queue is our commitment to the idea of 'cafness'. It's a word we made up. It's our North Star.

And to us it means this…

**Everyone is welcome. It's authenticity, nostalgia, community, simplicity and never getting too big for our boots.**

Cafs. Unassuming, unpretentious, honest, simple and authentic places to eat. They are a small slice of home, often run by families who throw their lives into making them a success. They don't pretend to do anything else. It's where we started and where we hope we will always be. The same goes for the food. We're not dealing in Michelin stars. It's bacon sandwiches, eggs and bubble and squeak. It's the Great British Breakfast, the full English, the full Monty and greasy spoons. It is our greatest culinary export found in places as far afield as Benidorm and Fuengirola. It doesn't get more 'national dish' than a full English.

Serves 2

# The Greasy Spoon

**Perfect for a weekday fry-up, perfect for a weekend 'sort me out' fry-up**

2 pork sausages
1tbsp vegetable oil
3 rashers streaky bacon
2 hash browns
2 fried eggs (see page 13)
100g baked beans

Preheat the oven to 200°C/180°C fan.

Put the sausages on a baking tray, drizzle with the oil and then roast them for 20–25 minutes, flipping halfway through, until golden and cooked through.

Meanwhile, put the bacon rashers on a baking tray, put another baking tray directly on top, to keep the rashers flat, and then put the hash browns on the top tray. Cook in the oven for 15–20 minutes until the bacon is golden brown and the hash browns crisp.

Put the fried eggs and beans on a plate and finish with the sausages, bacon and hash browns.

# Rise & Shine

**One for the veggies and vegans (remove the egg)**

1 portobello mushroom, thickly sliced
6 cherry tomatoes on the vine
Olive oil, for drizzling
Salt and pepper, to taste
1 portion of Pico de Gallo toast (page 115)
75g vegan chorizo, warmed
1 poached egg (see page 000)

Preheat the oven to 200°C/180°C fan.

Tip the mushroom slices and cherry tomatoes on the vine onto a baking tray, drizzle well with oil and season. Roast for 20–25 minutes, tossing the mushrooms halfway through, until softened.

Put the pico toast on a plate, then spoon on some of the vegan chorizo, the roasted mushrooms and tomatoes and finally add the poached egg.

Serves 1

# The Full Monty

*Everything you need is on this plate.
A proper caf classic*

Preheat the oven to 200°C/180°C fan.

Add the sausage, tomatoes, mushroom slices and hash brown to a baking tray, drizzle with 1 tablespoon of the oil and roast for 25–30 minutes, flipping the sausage and mushroom halfway through, until crisp, golden and cooked through.

Meanwhile, put the bacon rashers on a baking tray and put another baking tray directly on top, to keep the rashers flat. Cook in the oven for 15–20 minutes until the bacon is crisp and golden.

Heat the remaining oil in a small frying pan over a medium–high heat. Add the black pudding slice and cook for 1–2 minutes on each side until crisp.

Plate up time. Spoon the homestyle potatoes onto a plate, along with the roasted mushrooms, tomatoes, sausage and hash brown. Add on the bacon rashers, fried black pudding and fried eggs. Finish with the buttered toast and The Breakfast Club Beans.

1 sausage
6 cherry tomatoes on the vine
1 portobello mushroom, thickly sliced
1 hash brown
2 tbsp olive oil
2 rashers streaky bacon
1 slice black pudding
100g Homestyle Potatoes (page 124)
2 fried eggs (see page 13)
1 slice sourdough, toasted and buttered
100g The Breakfast Club Beans (page 120)

RELEASE YOUR INNER CAFNESS

Serves 1

# Veggie Spoon

**A caf-style fry-up, but 100% veggie**

Preheat the oven to 200°C/180°C fan.

Add the sausages, mushroom slices and tomatoes to a baking tray, drizzle with 1 tablespoon of the oil and then roast for 25–30 minutes, flipping the sausages and mushrooms halfway through, until golden and cooked through.

Heat the remaining oil in a frying pan over a medium heat and add the spinach. Season with salt and pepper and cook for 2–3 minutes until wilted.

Plate up time – put the fried egg on a plate and spoon on the beans. Add on the wilted spinach, sausages, mushrooms, tomatoes and crispy homestyle potatoes.

2 veggie sausages
1 portobello mushroom, thickly sliced
6 cherry tomatoes on the vine
2 tbsp olive oil
50g baby spinach
Salt and pepper, to taste
1 fried egg (see page 13)
100g The Breakfast Club Beans (page 120)
100g Homestyle Potatoes (page 124)

# Salt Beef Bubble & Squeak

**Serves 2**

You've got beef with us? We've got beef with you!

- 250g potato, peeled and cut into chunks
- 50g Salt Beef (page 120 or use shop bought) or pastrami, chopped
- 50g mature Cheddar cheese, coarsely grated
- 2 tbsp American or Dijon mustard
- 2 spring onions, thinly sliced
- A handful chives, finely chopped
- Salt and pepper, to taste
- 1tbsp vegetable oil, for frying
- Fried or poached eggs (see page 13), to serve

Fill a saucepan with salted cold water and add the peeled and chopped potatoes. Bring to the boil, reduce to a simmer and then cook for 12–15 minutes or until the potatoes are very tender when poked with the point of a knife.

Drain the potatoes really well and then mash. Leave to cool to room temperature.

Tip the cooled mash, chopped salt beef or pastrami, cheese, mustard, spring onions and chives into a bowl and season really well. Mix until everything is evenly combined and then form the mixture into 4 equal patties.

Chill for at least 10 minutes to firm up on a tray in the fridge. You could chill them overnight or even freeze them at this stage (defrost before cooking).

Preheat the oven to 200°C/180°C fan.

Heat a drizzle of oil in a large non-stick, oven-safe frying pan over a medium–high heat. Lay in the chilled patties and cook for 3–4 minutes until golden brown on the bottom. Flip and cook for another 3–4 minutes on the other side. Put into the oven for 5 minutes to heat through.

Serve with fried or poached eggs.

Serves 2

# Sweet Potato, Savoy Cabbage Bubble & Squeak

**Are you having a bubble?**

Tip the onion into a frying pan with the oil and a big pinch of salt and put over a medium–high heat. Cook, stirring regularly for 20 minutes.

Add the savoy cabbage and cook for a further 10 minutes, until the cabbage has wilted and the onion has completely softened and turned a deep caramel colour.

Preheat the oven to 200°C/180°C fan.

Tip the sweet potato onto a baking tray, drizzle with a little more oil and season well. Add the garlic cloves to the tray along with the thyme sprigs and roast for 20–25 minutes, tossing halfway through, until cooked through and a little caramelised.

Fill a saucepan with salted cold water and add the peeled and chopped potatoes. Bring to the boil, reduce to a simmer and then cook for 12–15 minutes or until tender. Drain the potatoes really well and then mash. Leave to cool to room temperature.

Tip the cooled mash [see p 62] into a bowl with the roasted sweet potato, then use a fork to roughly mash the roasted garlic cloves. Scrape in the caramelised onion and savoy cabbage mix and finally add the chives. Season really well and then form into 4 equal patties. Chill for at least 10 minutes to firm up.

Heat a drizzle of oil in a large non-stick frying pan over a medium–high heat. Lay in the patties and cook for 3–4 minutes until golden brown on the bottom. Flip and cook for another 3–4 minutes on the other side. Put into the oven for 5 minutes to heat through.

Serve with fried or poached eggs.

1 onion, thinly sliced
2 tbsp olive oil, plus extra for drizzling and frying
Salt and pepper, to taste
100g savoy cabbage, shredded
125g sweet potato, peeled and cut into 3cm dice
2 garlic cloves
A few thyme sprigs
125g potato, peeled and cut into chunks
A handful chives, finely chopped
Fried or poached eggs (see page 13), to serve

# The Perfect Bacon Roll

**Serves 1**

### We Built This City On Bacon Rolls

3 rashers streaky bacon
3 rashers back bacon
Knob of butter
1 breakfast roll, halved horizontally

**BREAKFAST SAUCE**
Ketchup
Brown sauce
Hot sauce

Heat a large non-stick frying pan over a medium–high heat and lay in the bacon rashers and add a splash of water. Cook for 6–8 minutes, turning the bacon halfway until the water has evaporated and the bacon rashers are crisp.

Remove the bacon from the pan, and add a knob of butter. Put the roll, cut sides down into the pan to fry and toast for a minute until golden.

Load the roll with the bacon slices and breakfast sauce, which is half ketchup half brown sauce with a few splashes of hot sauce.

65 **Cafness**

# Bacon, Avocado & Applewood Sandwich

**Serves 1**

**The Virgin Mary Mayo makes it. Slather it on**

- 3 rashers streaky bacon
- 1 hash brown
- 1 tbsp vegetable oil, for drizzling
- 1 brioche bun, halved horizontally and toasted
- 2 tbsp Virgin Mary Mayo (page 128)
- ½ jalapeño, sliced
- 1 slice Applewood smoked Cheddar cheese
- ½ avocado, peeled, destoned and crushed
- 2 tbsp Pink Pickled Onions (page 126)

Preheat the oven to 200°C/180°C fan.

Put the bacon rashers on a baking tray, along with the hash brown. Put another tray on top and press firmly to flatten the hash brown. Remove the tray, drizzle the hash brown with the oil, then put the tray back on top, to keep everything flat. Cook in the oven for 15–20 minutes until the bacon is golden brown and the hash brown is crisp.

Put the toasted bun halves on a plate and spread each cut side with 1 tablespoon of the mayo. On the bottom half on the bun, lay on the jalapeño slices, then the cheese slice, the avocado and then the pickled onions. Top with the smashed, crispy hash brown and bacon rashers, then top with the bun lid.

# Posh Sausage Sandwich

**What (I bet) Posh Spice makes for Sunday brunch**

Serves 1

Tip the onion into a frying pan with the oil and a big pinch of salt and put over a medium–high heat. Cook, stirring regularly, for 30 minutes until the onion has completely softened and turned a deep caramel colour.

Preheat the oven to 200°C/180°C fan.

Put the sausages on a roasting tray and cook in the oven for 20–25 minutes, turning halfway through, until they are golden and cooked through.

Turn the oven to the high grill setting.

Cut the sausages in half but not all the way through, so they are butterflied open. Put them back on the tray, cut side up. Lay the cheese slices over them and grill for a minute or until melted and bubbling.

Put the base of the toasted and buttered roll or 1 slice of the sourdough toast on a plate and top with the cheesy sausages. Top with the caramelised onion and a good spoonful of the chilli tomato chutney and then add the bun lid or other slice of sourdough toast.

- 1 onion, thinly sliced
- 3 tbsp olive oil
- Salt
- 2 sausages
- 2 slices Applewood smoked Cheddar cheese
- 1 breakfast roll, halved horizontally or 2 slices sourdough, toasted and buttered
- 1 tbsp chilli tomato chutney

Serves 1

# The Breakfast Club Burger

**The ultimate breakfast burger**

2 rashers streaky bacon
2 sausages
1 tbsp vegetable oil
1 brioche bun, halved horizontally and toasted
Ketchup, for spreading
2 slices American cheese
1 fried egg (see page 13 for our perfect frying guide)

Preheat the oven to 200°C/180°C fan.

Put the bacon rashers on a baking tray and put another baking tray directly on top, to keep the rashers flat. Cook in the oven for 15–20 minutes until the bacon is golden brown.

Remove the sausages from their skins and tip the meat into a bowl. Use slightly damp hands to form the meat into a 1cm thick patty, slightly wider than the width of your bun. Heat the oil in a non-stick frying pan over a medium heat and cook the patty for 3 minutes on each side until golden and cooked through.

Put the toasted bun halves on a plate, cut side up and spread with ketchup. Lay the 2 slices of cheese on the base and then put the sausage patty on top. Lay on the bacon and then top with the fried egg and finally the brioche bun lid.

Serves 1

# Avo, Egg & Cheese

*Avo - good, egg - good, cheese - good. avo, egg and cheese - delicious*

Crack the eggs into a bowl and use a whisk to break up and combine them until they are smooth and mixed.

Put a non-stick frying pan over a low heat and add the butter. Once the butter is foaming, pour the eggs into the pan. Swirl the egg around the pan to create a thin, even layer of egg.

Leave to cook for a minute, until the egg is three-quarters cooked but still a little wet on top. Carefully fold the omelette in half to create a semi-circle, then in half again.

Spread the top and bottom of the toasted bun with the mayo. On the base, lay on the cheese slice, the pink pickled onions, the crushed avo and the chopped sun-dried tomatoes. Lay on the omelette and finally add the top of the bun.

If you want to give this the final The Breakfast Club flourish, heat another frying pan over a medium heat and, once hot, put the sandwich into the pan, base first. Spoon a couple of tablespoons of water around the sandwich, then put a heatproof bowl over the top and leave to steam for 1 minute. Use a spatula to carefully lift the bowl, then remove. Serve the sandwich.

2 eggs (as fresh as possible!)
Knob of butter
1 brioche bun, halved horizontally and toasted
2 tbsp Chipotle & Harissa Mayo (page 128)
1 slice red Leicester cheese
3 tbsp Pink Pickled Onions (page 126)
½ avocado, peeled, destoned and roughly crushed
3 sun-dried tomatoes, drained and chopped

**Makes 6**

# Chorizo & Cheddar Sausage Rolls

**A Chef Matt sausage surprise. This is a good one for Christmas**

Remove the sausages and chorizo from their skins and squeeze the meat into a bowl along with the grated Cheddar, caramelised onions and some seasoning. Mix until everything is evenly incorporated.

Unroll the puff pastry on a clean work surface with the long side facing you. Cut the sheet in half horizontally, so you have 2 long strips of pastry.

Use slightly damp hands to shape half of the sausage meat into a long, even sausage that runs along the centre of one of the sheets of pastry, then repeat with the other half.

Fold the pastry over the sausage meat to encase it and use a fork to crimp and seal the pastry shut.

Brush the rolls with the beaten egg and sprinkle with the nigella seeds. Cut each roll into 3 pieces, so you have 6 in total. Line 2 baking trays with baking paper and put the sausage rolls on them with a gap between each. Chill for 20 minutes.

Meanwhile, preheat the oven to 200°C/180°C fan.

Bake the sausage rolls for 18–20 minutes or until puffed, golden and cooked through.

**These will keep, in an airtight container in the fridge, for 4 days.**

4 pork sausages (about 300g)
100g cooking chorizo
100g mature Cheddar cheese, coarsely grated
75g Caramelised Onions (page 126)
Salt and pepper, to taste
320g roll puff pastry
1 egg, beaten
2 tsp nigella seeds

# Chicken Kiev Sandwich

**It shouldn't work. But it really, really does**

Serves 1

1 chicken kiev
25g frozen peas
Olive oil, for drizzling
Salt and pepper, to taste
25g baby spinach
1 ciabatta roll, halved horizontally and toasted
50g Cheese Sauce (page 122), warmed
50g Burnt Onion Cream (page 126)

Cook the chicken kiev according to the packet instructions.

Tip the frozen peas into a frying pan with a drizzle of olive oil and put over a medium heat. Season with salt and pepper. Once the peas have defrosted use a fork to mash and crush them. Add in the baby spinach and continue to cook until it has wilted.

Put the toasted ciabatta halves on a plate, cut side up. Spoon the peas and spinach onto the base. Top with the chicken kiev, then spoon over the cheese sauce. Top with the burnt onion cream and then put on the ciabatta lid.

We recommend moving the sandwich to a piece of baking paper, then tightly wrapping up the sandwich before cutting it in half and devouring.

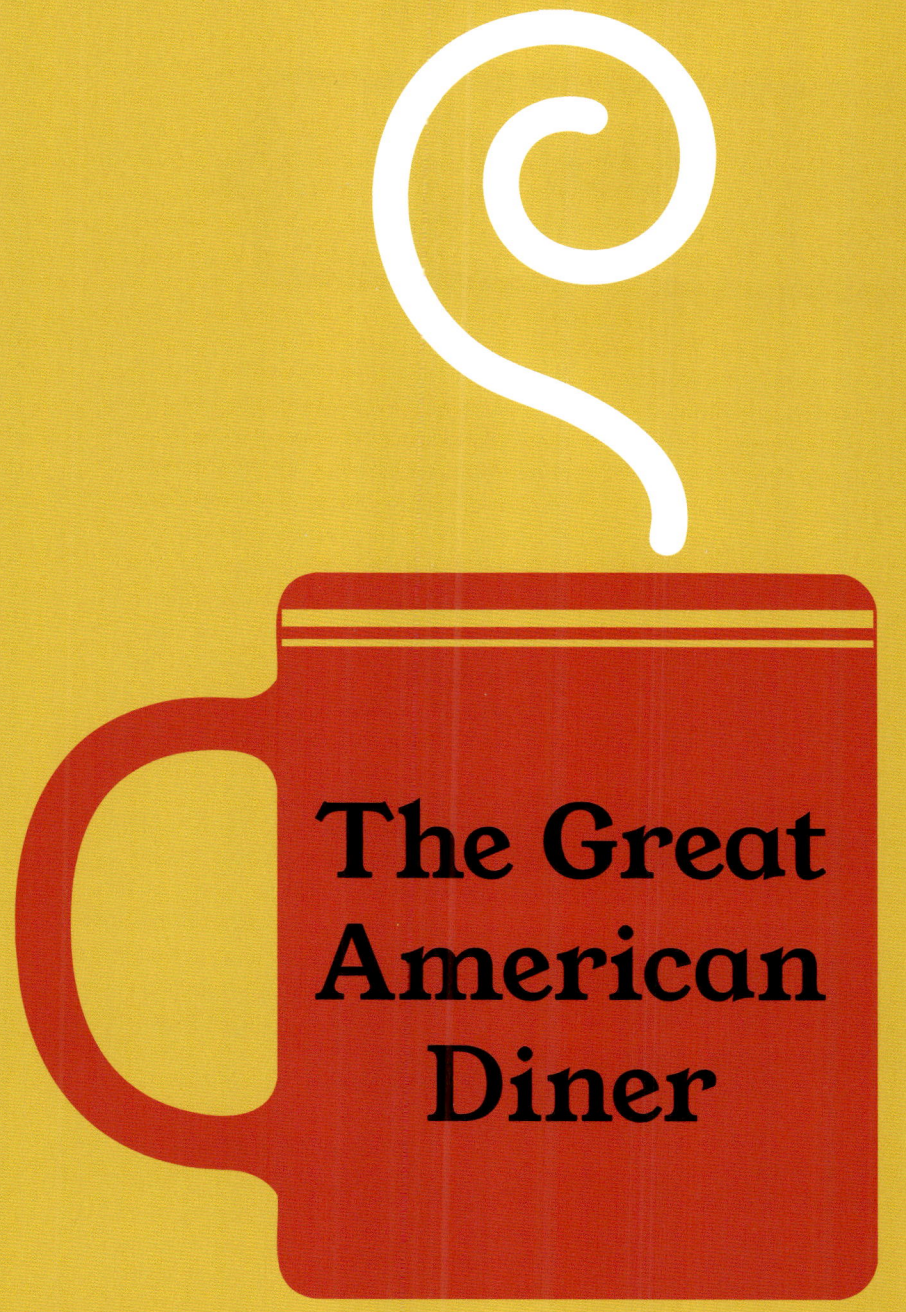

# TODAY
## is going to be a good day

These eight words can be found somewhere in all our cafs. Painted above a shopfront, in neon above our kitchens, across the top of our menus or behind one of our bars. Maybe it's a little bit of the American influence on The Breakfast Club. There's a certain unabashed 'have a nice day' positivity that's allowed in the US that we're slightly reticent about in the UK.

As well as being a superfan of their food, I have always been a huge admirer of the US approach to hospitality. It's full of warmth, care and a genuine desire to put a smile on your face. And what's wrong with a bit of positivity?! For most of our customers, we are the first port of call in their day, so let's make it a good start.

There is a story that perfectly sums this up. There was a was a lovely old Irishman called Mr Lee who used to clean the market stalls next to our caf in Angel. Every morning, first thing, whatever the weather, he'd be there tidying, making sure everything was spick and span for the market traders. He never complained and was always smiling, always ready to tell a joke, always ready to chat.

There were two girls working at the caf at the time, Meg and Kelly. One Saturday morning they came in an hour early and found the market-stall area in its usual post-Friday night state – bottles of beer, half-eaten kebabs and a whole host of other things. Meg and Kelly began scrubbing, mopping and cleaning, so when Mr Lee arrived the market-stall area was gleaming. It's rumoured he shed a tear. It didn't end there. The girls then asked him into the caf where a table had been laid for him. On it was a full English breakfast and a big glass of bubbly. That day was most definitely a good day for Mr Lee.

That's why I love what I do. There are so many wonderful stories every day, so many wonderful people, so much positivity, so much kindness. In hospitality we are in the business of kindness and looking after people. I know today is not always going to be a good day, sometimes it's a shitty day, but if we can help make it a better day our job is done.

The following pages are an ode to the US-inspired influence on the food we serve at The Breakfast Club. An ode to positivity and an ode to 'today is going to be a good day'. Just remember, the secret ingredient is always a smile. Food always tastes better when it's made with a smile.

Serves 1

# Grilled Cheese

This is the recipe for our classic Grilled Cheese, but you can add what you like to make it your own. We love adding harissa, Pink Pickled Onions, crispy bacon or even crispy fried chorizo (page 126)

Lay the slices of bread on a chopping board, so what will be the outsides of the sandwich are facing up. Spread both with the softened butter, then flip and load one slice with the grated cheese, then lay on the American cheese slices. Sandwich the other slice of bread, with the butter on the outside, on top.

Put a frying pan over a medium–high heat. Put the sandwich into the pan and then put another frying pan on top to weigh it down. This ensures flat, even contact with the pan, so more crispness! Fry for 3 minutes until really golden brown then flip, place the pan back on top and fry for a further 3 minutes on the other side.

2 slices sourdough
30g butter, softened
200g cheese, grated (we like a blend of Cheddar, red Leicester and mozzarella)
3 slices American cheese

**Serves 1**

# Disco Fries

**Could this be John Travolta's post-Saturday night, boogie woogie breakfast?**

150g frozen French fries
Salt and pepper, to taste
2 tsp rose harissa
60g Cheese Sauce (page 122), warmed
30g Mojo Picón (page 127)
½ jalapeño, thinly sliced
2 tbsp Pink Pickled Onions (page 126)
3 tbsp Pickled Red Cabbage (page 126)
2 tbsp Chimichurri (page 127)
1 spring onion, thinly sliced
Coriander leaves, to taste
1 fried egg (see page 13), to serve

Cook the frozen French fries according to the packet instructions. (Frozen French fries are also amazing deep-fried – straight from frozen!) Tip into a bowl and season well.

Put the fries on a serving platter or plate. Whisk the rose harissa into the cheese sauce and drizzle over the fries. Spoon over the mojo Picón, then dot with the jalapeño slices, pink pickled onions and pickled red cabbage. Drizzle over the chimichurri and scatter with the spring onion and coriander leaves. Top with a fried egg and serve.

81 **The Great American Diner**

Serves 2

# Homemade Hash Browns

**The GOAT side dish. Crispy, golden and goes with EVERYTHING**

4 potatoes, peeled and coarsely grated
1 onion, coarsely grated
20g cornflour
1 egg yolk
A handful chives, finely chopped
Salt and pepper, to taste
Vegetable oil, for frying

Tip the grated potatoes and onion into a clean tea towel and twist and squeeze to remove as much moisture as possible from them.

Tip into a bowl with the cornflour, egg yolk and chives and plenty of salt and pepper. Mix well.

Put a large non-stick frying pan over a medium–high heat and pour in enough of the oil to fill it 5mm deep.

Spoon in the hash brown mixture, making 12cm rounds that are roughly 2cm thick. Fry for 2–3 minutes on each side until golden brown and crispy. Place on kitchen paper to drain and season with salt.

Serves 1

# Breakfast Burrito

**A Breakfast Club classic. Make yours with chicken, chorizo or our housemade Vegan Chorizo (page 119)**

Put the tortilla on a board or plate. Spread over the soured cream in a thick line in the centre, leaving a gap at both ends. Top with the Cheddar, avocado, hot rice, pico de gallo, jalapeño slices and chicken or chorizo, if using.

Fold in both sides of the tortilla, then roll up to seal.

Lay a piece of foil on a work surface, then put the burrito on top. Fold in both sides and roll up to secure, then cut in half.

1 large flour tortilla
3 tbsp soured cream
50g Cheddar cheese, grated
½ avocado, peeled, destoned and roughly crushed
100g Mexican rice pouch, heated
4 tbsp Pico de Gallo (page 127)
3–4 slices pickled jalapeño
Sliced cooked chicken or chorizo (optional), to taste

**The Great American Diner**

# Cornflake Crusted Fire Wings

**Serves 1**

**Spicy wings coated in a classic breakfast cereal**

50g plain flour
2 eggs, beaten
80g cornflakes, crushed
6 chicken wings
Vegetable oil, for deep-frying
80ml St Elmo Wing Sauce (page 131)
1 tbsp Pickled Red Cabbage (page 126)
1 tbsp Pink Pickled Onions (page 126)
1 tbsp Pico de Gallo (page 127)
1 spring onion, thinly sliced

**TO SERVE**
A handful coriander leaves
Pickled chillies, to taste

Put the plain flour, beaten eggs and crushed cornflakes into 3 separate shallow bowls. Dredge the chicken wings first through the flour, then the beaten eggs and finally in the cornflakes, really patting to stick the cornflakes and fully coat the chicken.

Fill a saucepan half full with the vegetable oil and put over a medium–high heat. Line a shallow bowl with kitchen paper. Use a digital thermometer to heat the oil to 150°C. Carefully lower the chicken pieces into the oil and cook for 6 minutes until deeply golden brown and the chicken is cooked through. Use a slotted spoon to carefully lift the fried chicken onto the kitchen paper to drain any excess oil, and then tip them into a bowl.

Pour in the wing sauce and toss to fully coat.

Tip onto a platter and scatter over the pickled cabbage, pickled onions, pico de gallo and spring onion. Finish with coriander leaves and pickled chillies to serve.

Serves 2

# Fried Chicken Escalopes

**Perfect for stuffing in a sarnie or adding on the side of a Huevos Rancheros**

Put the chicken breast on a chopping board, then use a sharp knife to carefully cut the chicken in half horizontally into 2 thin pieces of the same shape.

Put the plain flour, beaten eggs and panko breadcrumbs into 3 separate shallow bowls.

Put the chicken pieces first into the flour, then the beaten egg and finally the panko breadcrumbs, really patting them to stick on the breadcrumbs.

Fill a saucepan half full with the vegetable oil and put over a medium–high heat. Line a shallow bowl with kitchen paper. Use a digital thermometer to heat the oil to 175°C. Carefully lower the chicken pieces into the oil and cook for 2–3 minutes until they are deeply golden brown and the chicken is cooked through. Use a slotted spoon to carefully lift the fried escalopes onto the kitchen paper to drain any excess oil.

Season with flaky sea salt.

1 chicken breast
50g plain flour
2 eggs, beaten
75g panko breadcrumbs
Vegetable oil, for deep-frying
Flaky sea salt, to taste

Winner winner chicken dinner

Serves 2

# Buttermilk Fried Chicken

**Winner winner chicken dinner**

4 skinless, boneless chicken thighs
300ml buttermilk
120g plain flour
2 tbsp cornflour
Big pinch cayenne pepper
½ tsp garlic powder
½ tsp onion powder
1 tsp smoked paprika
½ tsp dried thyme
Flaky sea salt and cracked black pepper, to taste
Vegetable oil, for deep-frying

Tip the chicken into a bowl and pour over the buttermilk. Mix really well to combine, then cover and chill for at least 4 hours but preferably overnight.

Mix together the plain flour and cornflour with all of the spices and herbs and plenty of salt and cracked black pepper.

Drain the chicken from the buttermilk, shaking off as much marinade as possible, then tip into the spiced flour mix. Dredge and pat to thickly coat each chicken piece in the flour.

Fill a saucepan half full with the vegetable oil and put over a medium–high heat. Line a shallow bowl with kitchen paper. Use a digital thermometer to heat the oil to 150°C. Carefully lower the chicken pieces into the oil and cook for 6 minutes until deeply golden brown and the chicken is cooked through. Use a slotted spoon to carefully lift the fried chicken onto the kitchen paper to drain the excess oil.

Season with flaky sea salt.

# Jonnie's Mac & Cheese

**Founder Jonnie's legendary Mac & Cheese, with a crunchy cornflake crust**

Serves 4

Preheat the oven to 200°C/180°C fan.

Heat the butter in a frying pan with the bacon lardons over a medium–high heat. Cook, stirring, for 5–8 minutes or until the lardons are super crisp and the fat has melted from them. Use a slotted spoon to scoop the lardons into a bowl.

Reduce the heat to low–medium and add the sliced leeks along with a large pinch of salt. Cook gently, stirring every now and again, for 10 minutes until soft, then add the garlic and cook for another 2 minutes. Scrape into the bowl with the lardons.

Cook the macaroni in a large pan of boiling salted water according to the packet instructions until al dente and still a little firm. Drain really well and run under cold running water until cooled, and then drain again. Tip into a separate large bowl.

Spoon the paprika into the bowl with the pasta, then pour in the milk and cream, along with 125g of the Parmesan, 200g of the mozzarella and 100g of the red Leicester. Spoon in the mustard, Worcestershire sauce and plenty of salt and pepper and mix well.

Into the bowl with the leeks and bacon add the panko breadcrumbs, cornflakes and remaining grated cheeses.

Scrape the pasta mix into a large baking dish, then evenly sprinkle over the cornflake topping. Scatter over a few chilli flakes, if using, then put the dish into the oven and bake for 25–30 minutes until golden and bubbling.

- 25g butter
- 200g bacon lardons
- 2 leeks, halved and thinly sliced
- Salt and pepper, to taste
- 3 garlic cloves, finely chopped
- 250g macaroni
- 2 tsp smoked paprika
- 250ml whole milk
- 450ml double cream
- 175g Parmesan cheese, finely grated
- 250g mozzarella, grated
- 150g red Leicester, finely grated
- 1½ tbsp Dijon mustard
- 2 tbsp Worcestershire sauce
- 30g panko breadcrumbs
- 30g cornflakes
- Big pinch dried chilli flakes (optional)

Serves 1

# The Breakfast Club Club

**Our Club Club is a classic, with a fresh herby aioli**

2 rashers streaky bacon
2 thick slices bread, toasted and buttered
4 tbsp Herb Aioli (page 128)
4 slices Fried Green Tomato (page 123)
30g cos lettuce, shredded
1 cooked chicken breast, sliced

Preheat the oven to 200°C/180°C fan.

Put the bacon rashers on a baking tray and put another baking tray directly on top, to keep the rashers flat. Cook in the oven for 15–20 minutes until the bacon is crisp and golden.

Spread both pieces of the toasted bread with the herb aioli, then top one with the 4 slices of fried green tomato. Add the bacon, then the shredded lettuce and the sliced chicken breast and then top with the other slice of toasted bread.

Cut diagonally through the corners to create 4 triangles.

Serves 1

# Reuben Sandwich

**Salty. Beefy. Mustardy. Phwoar**

Lay the slices of bread on a chopping board, so what will be the outsides of the sandwich are facing up. Spread both with the softened butter, then flip and spread the insides with the Reuben sauce. Top one with the Emmenthal slices, then the salt beef, sauerkraut and gherkin slices. Drizzle with mustard and add the other slice, with the butter on the outside, to sandwich the bread together.

Put a frying pan over a medium–high heat. Put the sandwich into the pan, then put another frying pan on top to weigh it down. This ensures a flat, even contact with the pan so more crispness! Fry for 3 minutes until really golden brown then flip, place the pan back on top and fry for a further 3 minutes on the other side.

Cut in half and serve with more gherkins and more Reuben sauce.

2 slices sourdough
30g butter, softened
4 tbsp Reuben Sauce (page 128), plus extra to serve
2 slices Emmenthal cheese
150g Salt Beef (page 120)
80g sauerkraut
2 gherkins, drained and sliced, plus extra to serve
2 tsp American mustard

Serves 1

# Philly Cheese Patty Melt

**A diner staple. Marrying a burger with a grilled cheese**

1 tbsp olive oil
125g burger patty
½ green pepper, deseeded and thinly sliced
15g Caramelised Onions (page 126)
2 slices sourdough
30g butter, softened
60g Cheddar cheese, grated
3 slices American cheese
60ml nacho cheese sauce
1 tbsp American mustard
Pickled chillies, to serve

Heat the olive oil in a frying pan over a medium–high heat. Put the patty in the pan, along with the green pepper slices, carefully squashing the patty down in the pan to flatten it. Cook for 2–3 minutes on each side until the patty is really golden, and then use a spoon to break the patty into small pieces. Continue frying for another few minutes until the patty is crisp and cooked through. Mix the caramelised onions into this and keep warm.

Lay the slices of bread on a chopping board, so what will be the outsides of the sandwich are facing up. Spread both with the softened butter, then flip and top one with the grated cheese, then lay on the American cheese slices. Top with the fried burger, peppers and onions, and mustard, then drizzle with the nacho cheese sauce. Top with the other slice of bread, with the butter on the outside.

Give the frying pan a wipe, then put it back over a medium–high heat. Put the sandwich into the pan, then put another frying pan on top to weigh it down. This ensures flat, even contact with the pan, so more crispness! Fry for 3 minutes until really golden brown then flip, put the pan back on top and fry for a further 3 minutes on the other side.

Cut in half and then serve with pickled chillies.

Serves 1

# Pulled Pork Sandwich

**Not seen on a menu since 2009. One for the nostalgia**

2 slices sourdough
30g butter, softened
200g c heese, grated (we like a blend of Cheddar, red Leicester and mozzarella)
150g Beer Pulled Pork (page 000)
3 slices American cheese

Lay the slices of bread on a chopping board, so what will be the outsides of the sandwich are facing up. Spread both with the softened butter, then flip and load one with the grated cheese, the pulled pork and then the American cheese slices Top with the other slice of bread, with the butter on the outside.

Put a frying pan over a medium–high heat. Put the sandwich in the pan, then put another frying pan on top to weigh it down. This ensures flat, even contact with the pan, so more crispness! Fry for 3 minutes until really golden brown then flip, put the pan back on top and fry for a further 3 minutes on the other side.

Serves 1

# Salt Beef Hash

**Meat and potatoes The Breakfast Club style**

Heat the olive oil in a large frying pan over a medium–high heat. Add in the salt beef and cook for 3–4 minutes until starting to crisp, then add the caramelised onions and homestyle potatoes. Fry for another few minutes and then add the pickled pink onions, red cabbage and pickled chillies. Toss to combine.

Spoon onto a large plate, top with the fried egg and pancakes and then drizzle with maple syrup to serve.

2 tbsp olive oil
100g Salt Beef (page 120), torn into pieces
40g Caramelised Onions (page 126)
200g Homestyle Potatoes (page 124)
40g Pickled Pink Onions (page 126)
50g Pickled Red Cabbage (page 126)
2 pickled chillies, sliced
1 fried egg (see page 13)
3 Classic Pancakes (page 39)
Maple syrup, to serve

Serves 1

# Crunchy Nut French Toast

100ml Vanilla French Toast Mix (page 134)
1 thick slice brioche or white bread
100g crunchy honey nut cornflakes

**TO SERVE (OPTIONAL)**
Caramelised banana (from the Bananaganza on page 49)
Peanut butter, to taste
Jam, to taste

Heat the oven to 200°C/180°C fan.

Put the vanilla French toast mix into a container and add in the brioche. Leave to soak for 2 minutes, turning halfway through.

Tip the cornflakes onto a baking tray, then lift the bread out of the custard mix and on the tray. Pat and coat the bread with the cornflakes until completely covered.

Put on a new baking tray and then bake for 8 minutes until caramelised and crisp.

Serve with caramelised banana, peanut butter and jam, if you like.

# Classic French Toast

100ml Vanilla French Toast Mix (page 134)
1 thick slice brioche or white bread
Knob of butter

**TO SERVE (OPTIONAL)**
Cherry Compote (page 135)
Vanilla Cream (page 132)

Put the vanilla French toast mix into a container and add in the brioche. Leave to soak for 2 minutes, turning halfway through.

Heat the knob of butter in a non-stick frying pan over a medium–high heat. Carefully drain the bread from the custard and lay in the hot pan. Cook for 2 minutes on each side until golden.

Serve with cherry compote and vanilla cream, if you like.

**Serves 1**

# Passion fruit Cheesecake Waffle

**Rich cheesecake cream topped with tangy passion fruit**

2 shop-bought waffles, warmed
1 passion fruit, halved
100g Passion Fruit Cheesecake Cream (page 134)
3 raspberries
Icing sugar, to serve

Put the waffles on a plate and spoon over half of the passion fruit seeds. Quenelle or spoon over the passion fruit cheesecake cream and then spoon over the remaining passion fruit seeds.

Place the raspberries on top and then dust with icing sugar to serve.

101 The Great American Diner

Welcome to the least expected chapter of The Breakfast Club book – the chapter where there's not an egg, bacon rasher or pancake in sight. From overnight oats to an absolutely banging breakfast sundae to a delicious, (and very healthy) banana split, these are the dishes for mornings that call for something a little lighter. It's time for your daily dose of rise and shine!

**Serves 2**

# Pineapple & Lime Overnight Oats

150ml whole milk (or plant based)
150g porridge oats
50g natural yogurt (or plant based)
Zest and juice of 1 lime, plus extra zest to serve
1 tbsp maple syrup
150g pineapple, diced, plus extra to serve
A splash pineapple juice
1 tbsp toasted coconut flakes

Add the milk, oats, yogurt, lime zest and juice, maple syrup, diced pineapple and pineapple juice to a bowl and mix really well. Cover the bowl, or put into a container, and chill overnight.

The next day, spoon the mixture into bowls and top with more diced pineapple, a grating of lime zest and the toasted coconut.

# Blueberry Overnight Oats

150ml whole milk (or plant based)
150g porridge oats
50g natural yogurt (or plant based)
50g apple, coarsely grated
50g Blueberry Compote (page 135), extra to serve
Zest and juice of 1 lemon

Add all of the ingredients to a bowl and mix really well. Cover the bowl, or put into a container, and chill overnight.

The next day, spoon the mixture into bowls and top with a little more blueberry compote.

# Maple Porridge

50g porridge oats
200ml whole milk (or plant based), extra to serve
1 tsp ground cinnamon, plus extra to serve
1 tbsp maple syrup, plus extra to serve
Chopped seasonal fruit, to serve

Tip the porridge oats, milk, cinnamon and maple syrup into a small saucepan and put over a medium heat. Cook, stirring, for 5 minutes until the porridge has thickened and is bubbling.

Scrape into a bowl, pour over a little more milk, place the chopped fruit over the top, dust with cinnamon and drizzle with maple syrup to serve.

Makes 1 loaf

# Banana Bread

This banana bread is great as is, or you can add in 200g dark chocolate chunks if you're a chocolate fiend!

Vegetable oil or butter, for greasing
4 very ripe bananas, peeled and mashed
60g runny honey
2 eggs
2 tsp vanilla extract
180g plain flour
2 tsp baking powder
1 tsp ground cinnamon
½ tsp fine sea salt

Preheat the oven to 180°C/160°C fan and grease a 1lb loaf tin.

Tip the mashed bananas into a bowl along with the honey, eggs and vanilla and whisk to combine.

Add in the remaining ingredients and fold together until evenly combined. Pour into the prepared tin and bake for 50–55 minutes or until a skewer inserted into the centre comes out clean.

Cool in the tin for 10 minutes, then turn out onto a wire rack and cool completely.

**If you can resist the extra slices, this will keep in a tin or airtight container for 3 days.**

Serves 1

# Banana Bread with Roasted Peaches

**Cake for breakfast?! Where do we sign?!**

Dust the bottom of a non-stick frying pan with the icing sugar and lay in the slices of peach, cut side down. Put over a high heat and cook for a few minutes until the peaches are starting to caramelise. Add the honey to the pan and toss and cook for another few minutes until the peaches are charred and glossy.

Spread the toasted banana bread with the yogurt, and then pile on the caramelised peach pieces. Sprinkle with the granola and toasted coconut flakes to finish.

1 tbsp icing sugar
1 peach, destoned and cut into 6 wedges
1 tbsp runny honey
1 slice Banana Bread (opposite), toasted
50g natural or coconut yogurt
1 tsp granola
2 tsp toasted coconut flakes

Rise & Shine

Serves 1

# Breakfast Sundae

**You could eat this Breakfast Sundae on a Sunday if you wanted...**

1½ passion fruit, halved
80g granola
100g natural or coconut yogurt
1 tbsp toasted coconut flakes

Scrape the seeds of 1 passion fruit into the bottom of a sundae glass, then top with a good sprinkling of the granola.

Spoon in three-quarters of the yogurt and then top with the remaining granola, a scoop more of the yogurt and finally the remaining passion fruit seeds and coconut flakes to finish.

# Guilt-Free Banana Split

**Healthy dessert at 8am**

Serves 1

Mix the diced pineapple together with the chilli flakes, lime zest and juice and 1 tablespoon of the honey or maple syrup in a small bowl. Cover and leave to marinate for at least 30 minutes but preferably overnight in the fridge.

Mix the yogurt with the passion fruit seeds and the remaining honey or maple syrup.

Put the banana halves on a plate, cut side up. Spoon on the yogurt, then the marinated pineapple. Sprinkle with coconut flakes and berries of your choice to serve.

80g pineapple, diced
Good pinch dried chilli flakes
Zest and juice of ½ lime
2 tbsp runny honey or maple syrup
50g natural yogurt
1 passion fruit, halved
1 banana, peeled and sliced lengthways
1 tbsp toasted coconut flakes, to serve
50g raspberries or blueberries

Serves 1

# Smashed Avo & Pico de Gallo Toast

**Avo look at this. Smashed avo toast & ours is served with a fiery orange mojo Picón sauce**

Spread the toasted sourdough with the Mojo Picón, right to the edges.

Spoon on the crushed avocado, then spoon over the pico de gallo. Sprinkle with the spring onicn to serve.

1 slice sourdough, toasted
2 tbsp Mojo Picón (page 127)
1 avocado, peeled, destoned and roughly crushed
1 tbsp Pico de Gallo (page 127)
½ spring onion, finely sliced, to serve

# Batch & Sauce

# Vegan Chorizo

*Serves 4*

3 tbsp olive oil
3 garlic cloves, finely chopped
250g vegan mince
2 tbsp rose harissa
2 tbsp tomato purée
60g sundried tomatoes, drained and finely chopped
1 tsp smoked paprika
1 tbsp garlic powder
½ tsp ground cumin
½ tsp hot chilli powder
½ tsp dried oregano
Salt and pepper, to taste
Juice of ½ lemon

Heat the olive oil in a frying pan over a medium–high heat. Scrape in the garlic and cook, stirring, for 2 minutes until softened but not coloured. Add in the mince and toss, break it up and stir for 1 minute.

Spoon in the harissa, tomato purée and sundried tomato pieces and cook for 1 minute before adding all of the dried spices and herbs. Fry for a further 1 minute and then add 50ml of water.

Season, add the lemon juice and then cook for 1 minute or until thickened and glossy.

# Scrambled Tofu

*Serves 4*

280g pack firm tofu, drained and crumbled
2 tbsp tahini
75ml oat cream
2 tsp Dijon mustard
4 spring onions, thinly sliced
Salt and cracked black pepper, to taste
Juice of ½ lemon, or to taste
Finely chopped chives, to serve

Mix together the crumbled tofu, tahini, oat cream, mustard and spring onions with some salt and plenty of cracked black pepper in a bowl.

Squeeze in the lemon juice to taste.

Serves 4

# The Breakfast Club Beans

2 tbsp vegetable oil
1 onion, finely chopped
4 garlic cloves, finely chopped
Salt and pepper, to taste
1½ tbsp tomato purée
1 tsp hot smoked paprika
400g tin butter beans, drained
2 tsp soft brown sugar
1 tbsp soy sauce
1½ tbsp rose harissa
250g passata
1 tsp dried thyme

Heat the vegetable oil in a saucepan over a medium–high heat and add the onion and garlic along with a pinch of salt. Cook for 6–8 minutes until softened, then add the tomato purée and smoked paprika and cook for 2 minutes, stirring regularly.

Tip in the drained butter beans, sugar and soy sauce and mix well. Stir in the harissa and continue to cook everything for another 2 minutes before tipping in the passata and mixing well. Simmer gently for 10 minutes, stirring occasionally.

Stir in the dried thyme and season to taste.

**The beans will keep, covered, in the fridge for 4 days.**

# Salt Beef

1kg cured beef brisket (available to pre-order from your local butcher)
2 large onions, quartered
2 carrots, cut into large chunks
2 celery sticks, cut into large chunks
1 leek, cut into large chunks
2 bay leaves
10 black peppercorns
6 whole garlic cloves, peeled

Put the brisket and all the other ingredients into a large saucepan and pour over enough cold water to completely cover.

Put over a high heat and bring to a simmer, then reduce the heat and bubble gently for 3–4 hours until the meat is meltingly tender. Use a large spoon to scrape off any scum from the surface.

Drain and discard the liquid, then use the beef as desired.

Serves 4

# Beer Pulled Pork

**Meltingly tender and coated in a luscious bbq sauce**

Spoon all of the dry ingredients into a large bowl with a big pinch of salt and pepper and mix well. Spoon in the mustard and ketchup, mix again, then pour in the beer and white wine vinegar. Add in the pork and mix until it is completely coated. Chill for at least 4 hours but preferably overnight.

When you are ready to cook, preheat the oven to 200°C/180°C fan.

Put the pork and all the marinade into a roasting tray and cover with a layer of baking paper, and then foil. Roast in the oven for 20 minutes.

Reduce the heat to 160°C/150°C fan and cook for 2 hours 30 minutes or until the pork is meltingly tender.

Drain the pork cooking liquid into a saucepan and whisk in the bbq sauce ingredients. Bring to the boil, reduce the heat to a simmer and then simmer for about 10 minutes until the sauce has reduced and you get a thick, luscious sauce.

Shred the pork and mix it into the sauce.

**This will keep, covered, in the fridge for 3 days.**

2 tsp garlic powder
1 tsp dried chilli flakes
4 tbsp soft light brown sugar
2 tsp dried mixed herbs
1 tbsp paprika
2 tsp ground cumin
Salt and pepper, to taste
1 tbsp Dijon mustard
4 tbsp ketchup
500ml lager
2 tbsp white wine vinegar
1.5kg skinless, boneless pork shoulder, cut into 6cm pieces

**BBQ SAUCE**
4 tbsp ketchup
2 tbsp Dijon mustard
1 tbsp apple cider vinegar
1 tbsp soft light brown sugar
1 tsp Worcestershire sauce

Serves 4

# Cheese Sauce

25g butter
25g plain flour
325ml whole milk
100g red Leicester cheese, coarsely grated
100g American cheese slices
50g Grana Padano or Parmesan cheese, finely grated
Big pinch cayenne pepper, or more to taste
Salt and pepper, to taste

Melt the butter in a saucepan over a medium heat and, once the butter is foaming, add in the flour and cook, stirring, for a few minutes until it becomes a smooth paste. Add a quarter of the milk, and then stir and beat the mixture until it is completely combined and smooth, then add another quarter and repeat. Do this twice more until you have used all the milk and you have a silky smooth sauce.

Add in all of the cheeses along with the cayenne pepper. Whisk for a minute or two until the cheeses have completely melted, then remove from the heat. Season with salt and pepper, and more cayenne, if you like.

**This will keep, with the surface covered with clingfilm, in the fridge for 5 days.**

# Beer Cheese

150ml lager or pale ale
200g Cheddar cheese, finely grated
50g American cheese slices
½ tsp smoked paprika
½ tsp cayenne pepper
Salt and pepper, to taste

Pour the beer into a saucepan and bring to the boil. Add in both cheeses and whisk to a smooth, thick sauce. Spoon in the paprika and cayenne and season to taste.

# Fried Green Tomatoes

Serves 1

The tomatoes used for this are slightly underripe and therefore green, meaning they hold their shape when fried but still have all that delicious tomato flavour

Put the seasoned flour, beaten egg and breadcrumbs into 3 separate shallow bowls. Take a tomato slice and coat it in the flour, then the egg and finally the breadcrumbs, patting to coat and stick the breadcrumbs on. Put on a baking tray and you repeat with the rest of the tomato slices.

Fill a saucepan half full with the vegetable oil and put over a medium–high heat. Line a shallow bowl with kitchen paper. Use a digital thermometer to heat the oil to 180°C. Working in batches, carefully lower a few of the breaded tomato slices into the hot oil and cook for 1 minute or until golden brown and crisp. Use a slotted spoon to carefully lift the tomato slices out of the oil and then drain on the kitchen paper. Season with salt.

100g plain flour, seasoned with salt and pepper
3 eggs, beaten
100g panko breadcrumbs
3 green tomatoes, cut into 1cm thick slices
Vegetable oil, for deep frying

Serves 4

# Homestyle Potatoes

**In our restaurants we deep-fry these for extra crispness, but we've changed up the method to make these a little more home friendly**

4 large potatoes (like Maris Piper or King Edward), peeled and cut into 3cm cubes
Salt
75ml vegetable oil

Preheat the oven to 200°C/180°C fan.

Tip the peeled potatoes into a saucepan of cold water with a big pinch of salt and put over a high heat. Bring to the boil and simmer for 5 minutes. Drain really well.

Pour the oil on a baking tray then add on the cubed potatoes. Roast for 30–40 minutes, tossing regularly, until super crisp and golden. Season with salt.

Serves 4

## Caramelised Onions

4 onions, very thinly sliced
4 tbsp olive oil
Salt

Tip the onions into a large frying pan with the oil and a big pinch of salt and put over a medium heat. Cook, stirring regularly, for 50–55 minutes until they have completely softened and turned a deep caramel colour.

## Pink Pickled Onions

4 red onions, thinly sliced
300ml white wine vinegar
100g caster sugar

Put the red onions in a heatproof bowl.

Heat the vinegar and sugar in a saucepan until the liquid is steaming and the sugar has fully dissolved.

Pour the vinegar and sugar mixture over the onions, cover and leave to cool. Chill until needed.

**Keeps, covered, in the fridge for 1 week.**

## Pickled Red Cabbage

½ red cabbage, very thinly sliced
Juice of 2 limes
Salt

Tip the finely sliced cabbage into a bowl and squeeze in the lime juice. Add in a big pinch of salt and use clean hands to massage the lime and salt into the cabbage.

Chill for at least 1 hour before serving – the cabbage will have softened slightly and turned a bright pink.

**Keeps, covered, in the fridge for 3 days.**

## Burnt Onion Cream

125g Caramelised Onions (above)
250ml double cream

Tip the caramelised onions into a saucepan, pour in the cream and put over a medium heat. Bring to a rapid boil and then remove from the heat. Pour into a container, cover the surface with clingfilm and chill completely before using.

Serves 4

# Mojo Picón

2 red chillies, deseeded and roughly chopped
4 garlic cloves, very roughly chopped
100ml vegetable oil
25g panko breadcrumbs
125g roasted red peppers from a jar, drained and chopped
1 tsp smoked paprika
A handful coriander
Big pinch cayenne pepper
2 tsp malt vinegar, or more to taste
Salt and pepper, to taste

Preheat the oven to 200°C/180°C fan.

Tip the chillies and garlic onto a baking tray and drizzle with a little of the oil. Cook in the oven for 10 minutes.

Tip the breadcrumbs onto a small baking tray, spread into an even layer and toast in the oven for 8 minutes.

Add the roasted chillies, and garlic and remaining ingredients except the toasted panko bread-crumbs and seasoning to a blender and whizz until completely smooth. Add in the panko and whizz again so you have a smooth, thick sauce. Season with salt and pepper, and a little more malt vinegar if you think it needs it.

**Keeps, covered, in the fridge for 1 week.**

# Chimichurri

4 garlic cloves
Large bunch coriander
Large bunch flat-leaf parsley
Zest and juice of 2 limes
100ml olive oil
Salt and pepper, to taste
1 red chilli, finely chopped
1 green chilli, finely chopped

Tip the garlic, coriander, parsley, lime zest and juice and olive oil into a blender with some salt and pepper and blend until finely chopped. Stir through the red and green chopped chillies.

**Keeps, covered, in the fridge for 3 days.**

# Pico de Gallo

1 red pepper, deseeded and finely diced
1 red onion, finely chopped
2 large, ripe tomatoes, seeds removed and finely diced
½–1 green chilli, deseeded and finely chopped
1 small garlic clove, crushed
A handful coriander, finely chopped
Juice of ½ lime
2 tsp agave syrup
Salt and pepper, to taste

Add all of the ingredients to a bowl, season and mix well.

**Keeps, covered, in the fridge for 3 days.**

Serves 4

# Virgin Mary Mayo

6 tbsp mayonnaise
6 tbsp ketchup
1 tbsp soy sauce
Good dash Tabasco

Spoon all of the ingredients into a bowl and mix together to combine.

# Reuben Sauce

4 tbsp ketchup
4 tbsp mayonnaise
1 tbsp horseradish sauce
1 tsp Tabasco
1 tsp Worcestershire sauce
1 shallot, finely chopped
2 gherkins, drained and finely chopped
Big pinch smoked paprika
A handful chives, finely chopped
Salt and pepper, to taste

Tip all of the ingredients into a bowl with a little salt and pepper and mix together. Taste and adjust to how you like it!

**Keep, in a container, in the fridge for 1 week.**

# Chipotle & Harissa Mayo

9 tbsp mayonnaise
3 tbsp chipotle paste
3 tbsp rose harissa

Mix the ingredients together in a small bowl.

# Herb Aioli

35g mixed herbs (parsley, dill, mint and basil work well)
Zest and juice of ½ lemon, or more juice to taste
1 small clove garlic, crushed
200g mayonnaise
Salt and pepper, to taste

Put the herbs into a blender and add the lemon zest and juice, crushed garlic and a big spoonful of the mayonnaise. Whizz until bright green and smooth.

Tip into a bowl and fold through the remaining mayonnaise. Taste for salt, pepper and lemon juice and adjust if needed.

Serves 4

# Chipotle & Tomato Sauce

Put the ancho chillies into a jug and pour over the boiled water. Leave for 20 minutes to soak.

Heat the olive oil in a saucepan over a medium–high heat. Scrape in the red onions along with a pinch of salt and cook for 6–8 minutes until the onions are beginning to soften, then scrape in the garlic and cook for another 1 minute.

Add the cumin, sugar, chopped peppers, drained beans, coriander and chipotle paste and cook for 5 minutes, stirring occasionally.

Carefully remove the ancho chillies from the soaking liquid (keep!), remove the stalks and roughly chop. Scrape into the saucepan, pour in the soaking liquid and add the plum tomatoes along with the bay leaves and red wine vinegar.

Bring to the boil, reduce the heat and simmer for 1 hour, stirring now and again, until thickened.

Remove the bay leaves. Pour the mixture into a blender blend to a thick, smooth sauce.

**Keeps, covered, in the fridge for 1 week.**

2 ancho chillies
500ml just-boiled water
4 tbsp extra-virgin olive oil
2 red onions, finely chopped
Salt
6 garlic cloves, finely chopped
1 tbsp ground cumin
2 tbsp caster sugar
3 roasted red peppers from a jar, drained and chopped
200g tinned black beans, drained
A handful coriander, chopped
5 tbsp chipotle in adobo paste
400g tin plum tomatoes
2 bay leaves
2 tbsp red wine vinegar

Serves 2

# Hollandaise

2 egg yolks
2 tsp white wine vinegar
225g clarified butter
Salt and pepper, to taste
Juice of 1 lemon
Pinch cayenne pepper

Fill a small saucepan with 5cm of boiling water and put over a low–medium heat. Put the egg yolks into a medium heatproof bowl with the white wine vinegar and 3 tablespoons of water. Whisk together briefly to combine.

Put the bowl on top of the simmering water – you want to make sure the bottom of the bowl is not in contact with the water. Reduce the heat to low as the bowl being on top of the water will act as a lid and increase the boiling rate and heat.

Whisk constantly for 2–3 minutes until the mixture has become paler and doubled in volume.

Remove the pan from the heat but leave the bowl on top of the pan. Whisk the clarified butter into the mixture, 1 tablespoon at a time, only adding more once the last tablespoon has been fully incorporated. Once all of the butter has been incorporated, season with salt, pepper and lemon juice. Finish with a pinch of cayenne and keep warm over the bowl, whisking regularly until needed.

**If your mixture splits, which is likely if the butter is added too quickly, add 1 teaspoon of boiling water to the mix and whisk well.**

**Makes 1kg**

# Dill Pickles

1kg baby cucumbers
150ml white wine vinegar
150g caster sugar
2 red chillies, sliced
4 garlic cloves, chopped
Small bunch dill, roughly chopped
Salt and pepper, to taste

Slice the cucumbers into long 1cm batons.

Pour the vinegar into a container or bowl and add the sugar, chillies, garlic and dill. Season with salt and pepper and then whisk together to combine.

Add the cucumbers into the container, cover and chill for at least a few hours.

**Keeps, covered, in the fridge for 2 weeks.**

**Makes loads**

# Wing Sauce

180ml hot sauce – we love Frank's
50g butter, melted
2 tbsp sriracha
50ml barbecue sauce
2 tsp Worcestershire sauce
2 tsp runny honey

Whisk all of the ingredients together in a bowl.

Serves 4

## Cherry Cream

600ml Vanilla Cream (opposite)
100g Cherry Compote (135)

Spoon the vanilla cream into a bowl and then spoon in the compote. Use a large spoon to ripple the compote through the cream.

## Blueberry Cream

600ml Vanilla Cream (opposite)
100g Blueberry Compote (page 135)

Spoon the vanilla cream into a bowl and then spoon in the compote. Use a large spoon to ripple the compote through the cream.

## Vanilla Cream

600ml double cream
2 tbsp icing sugar
2 tsp vanilla extract

Pour all of the ingredients into a bowl and whisk until it holds soft peaks.

**Keeps, covered, in the fridge for 3 days.**

## Lemon Cream

600ml double cream
2 tbsp icing sugar
2 tsp vanilla extract
Zest of ½ lemon

Pour all of the ingredients into a bowl and whisk until it holds soft peaks.

Serves 4

## Passion Fruit Cheesecake Cream

250g cream cheese
30g passion fruit purée
40g icing sugar
125ml double cream
1 passion fruit, halved

Put the cream cheese, passion fruit purée and icing sugar into a bowl and whisk until smooth. Pour in a quarter of the cream and whisk again.

Pour the remaining cream into a separate bowl and whisk until it just holds soft peaks.

Use a spatula to fold the 2 mixtures together.

Fold in the passion fruit seeds.

## Vanilla French Toast Mix

4 eggs
200ml whole milk
1 tsp vanilla extract

Whisk all of the ingredients together in a bowl.

## Chocolate Cream

50g dark chocolate, chopped
600ml Vanilla Cream (page 132)

Tip the chocolate into a heatproof bowl and melt in short pulses in the microwave, stirring in between, until fully melted.

Spoon the cream into a bowl, and then pour in the melted chocolate. Use a large spoon to ripple the chocolate through the cream.

## Cheesecake Cream

250g cream cheese
40g icing sugar
½ tsp vanilla extract
125ml double cream

Put the cream cheese, icing sugar and vanilla in a bowl and whisk until smooth. Pour in a quarter of the cream and whisk again.

Pour the remaining cream into a separate bowl and whisk until it can just hold soft peaks.

Use a spatula to fold the 2 mixtures together.

*Serves 4*

# Cherry Compote

500g frozen sour cherries or black cherries
50g icing sugar
Zest of 4 lemons

Tip all of the ingredients into a saucepan and put over a medium heat. Bring to the boil, stirring every now and again, and then reduce to a simmer. Bubble away gently, stirring regularly, for 20 minutes until most of the liquid has reduced.

Pour into a container and chill.

**Keeps, covered, in the fridge for 1 week; it also freezes really well.**

# Blueberry Compote

500g frozen blueberries
50g icing sugar
Zest of 4 lemons

Tip all of the ingredients into a saucepan and put over a medium heat. Bring to the boil, stirring every now and again, and then reduce to a simmer. Bubble away gently, stirring regularly, for 20 minutes until most of the liquid has reduced.

Pour into a container and chill.

**Keeps, covered, in the fridge for 1 week; it also freezes really well.**

# Salted Caramel & Chocolate Sauce

300ml double cream
2 x 180g salted caramel chocolate bars, chopped – We double love Tony's!
2 tbsp caramel sauce
1 tsp flaky sea salt

Pour the double cream into a small saucepan over a low–medium heat and gently bring to the boil while stirring.

Remove the pan from the heat and add the chopped chocolate. Leave for 30 seconds or so, and then gently stir until the chocolate has fully melted and incorporated.

Pour in the caramel sauce and salt and mix well.

**Keeps, with the surface covered with clingfilm, in the fridge for 5 days.**

# DRINKS

If you're ever in Spitalfields on an evening pop in to The Breakfast Club. The lights will be off, the caf will be closed. A member of staff will greet you like a long-lost friend, even if the security might not be so warm. Tell them: 'I'm here to see The Mayor'. They'll open the door of a seven-foot-high Smeg fridge in a corner of the caf and walk you in. They'll then proceed to run you through a few rules (pay attention) before heading down some secret stairs to the entrance of London's best—and worst—kept secret. A speakeasy bar full of cat references, delicious cocktails and not a mayor in sight.

Its full name, to be precise, is The Mayor of Scaredy Cat Town. It's a name that pays homage to an episode of Cheers as does our other speakeasy in London Bridge, Call Me Mr Lucky. It's safe to say our love of the sitcom … runs deep.

They have become pretty famous over the years, once winning London's Bar of The Year. While it's not so secret now, you still see jaws drop when the fridge opens and a crowd of people walk in.

The Mayor of Scaredy Cat Town is where we nurtured our love of cocktails. In 2005, if you were feeling adventurous, in the morning, you'd maybe push the boat out and have a Bloody Mary. Fast forward to brunch in 2025 and you'd be disappointed if your cocktails aren't bottomless, your bartender isn't a six-foot-four drag queen and 'Proud Mary' isn't blaring from the speakers. Dancing at breakfast time is something I would definitely recommend. Times have changed, big wheels keep on turning!

So while the classics are here – delicious Bloody Marys and Mimosas (or Bucks Fizz as I remember them) as well as some wonderfully creative cocktails that are great for whatever time of day you fancy them. Crank up the music in your kitchen, pour yourself a cocktail and get cooking, shaking and pouring.

Thank you to all the Mayors, past and present.

THE MAYOR OF SCAREDY CAT TOWN

### Serves 4

# Blood Mary Batch Mix

**Not just any Bloody Mary, a Breakfast Club Bloody Mary**

1 litre tomato juice
25ml sugar syrup
75ml Worcestershire sauce
5 dashes Tabasco
½ tsp celery salt, or more to taste
½ tsp pepper, or more to taste
2 tsp English mustard
Zest of 2 lemons
Zest of 2 oranges
25ml lemon juice
15ml lime juice

Pour all of the ingredients into a large jug or bowl and mix really well. Season and adjust with the seasoning to your liking.

**Keeps, covered, in the fridge for 1 week.**

### Serves 1

# The Breakfast Club Bloody Mary

1 lemon wedge
Salt or chip spice
Ice, for serving
200ml Bloody Mary mix (page 000)
50ml vodka
1 silverskin pickled onion
2 cornichons
1 pickled chilli
3 basil leaves

To spice things up, run the wedge of lemon around the rim of the glass and then dip the rim into the salt or chip spice.

Fill the glass with ice, and then add the bloody Mary mix and vodka.

Skewer the onion, cornichons and pickled chilli on a cocktail stick and lay across to the glass with the basil leaves. Lay on the lemon wedge and serve.

# Ruby Murray Mary

*Serves 2*

500ml tomato juice
2 tbsp Worcestershire sauce
2 tbsp Tabasco
1 garlic clove, finely grated
Thumb-sized piece of ginger, peeled and finely grated
½ red onion, chopped
200ml coconut milk
Zest and juice of 1 lime
1 tbsp hot madras curry powder
1 tbsp natural yogurt
Salt and cracked black pepper, to taste
Ice, for serving
50ml vodka

**TO SERVE**
Coriander sprigs
4 mini poppadoms
2 tsp mango chutney
2 bird's eye chilli

Tip the tomato juice, Worcestershire sauce, Tabasco, garlic, ginger, onion, coconut milk, lime zest and juice, curry powder and yogurt into a blender and whizz until smooth. Season with salt and cracked black pepper.

Fill a glass with ice and pour in the vodka. Pour 150ml of the bloody Mary mix into each glass and mix well. Garnish each drink with a coriander sprig, 2 mini poppadoms, a spoonful of mango chutney and a chilli.

# Greek Bloody Mary

*Serves 1*

¼ red onion, finely chopped
¼ bird's eye chilli
¼ cucumber, peeled and finely diced
1 kalamata olive
50ml vodka
150ml passata
1 tbsp extra-virgin olive oil
1 tbsp red wine
2 tsp Worcestershire sauce
2 tsp lemon juice
Salt and pepper, to taste
Ice, for serving

**TO SERVE**
1 small cube feta
1 cherry tomato
1 kalamata olive
1 cube cucumber
2 basil leaves
2 oregano leaves

Put the red onion, chilli, cucumber and olive into the bottom of a glass and muddle until completely pulverised.

Pour the remaining ingredients, except the ice, into a shaker and shake well.

Fill the glass with ice, pour in the drink and mix.

Put the feta, cherry tomato, olive and cucumber onto a cocktail stick, and lay across the top of the glass with basil and oregano leaves.

*Serves 1*

# Rise & Shine Mimosa

125ml prosecco
35ml orange juice
10ml pink grapefruit syrup or grenadine

Pour the prosecco into a champagne flute, followed by the orange juice. Finish with the syrup or grenadine to get a two-tone effect.

# Marmalade Margarita

50ml tequila
20ml triple sec
20ml lime juice
1 tsp agave syrup
2 tsp marmalade
2 twists of orange rind
Ice, for shaking

Put the tequila, triple sec, lime juice, agave syrup, marmalade and one of the orange rinds into a cocktail shaker. Fill with ice and shake vigorously.

Strain into a short, wide glass and garnish with the reserved twist of orange rind.

# Breakfast Mai Tai

25ml pineapple juice
25ml grapefruit juice
20ml orgeat (almond syrup)
20ml lime syrup
15ml triple sec
35ml white rum
Ice, for shaking and serving
35ml dark rum

**TO SERVE**
1 slice grapefruit
1 mint sprig
1 cocktail cherry

Pour both juices, the almond and lime syrups, triple sec and white rum into a cocktail shaker. (Don't worry; you're saving the dark rum for later.) Fill with ice and shake.

Fill a tall glass with ice and then strain in the shaken mix.

Pour the dark rum over the top.

Finish with a grapefruit slice, mint sprig and a cocktail cherry.

Serves 1

# Breakfast Negroni

50ml grapefruit gin
Ice for serving
50ml Aperol
50ml Martini Rosso
1 orange wedge or twist of rind, to serve

Pour the grapefruit gin into a short, wide glass filled with ice, along with the Aperol and Martini Rosso. Stir all together.

Finish with the orange wedge or twist.

If you don't have grapefruit gin to hand, you can a squeeze of fresh grapefruit to any dry gin.

# Morning Mojito

Crushed ice, for serving
10ml sugar syrup
35ml vodka
4 mint leaves, plus a sprig to serve
75ml grapefruit juice
1 lemon wedge, to serve

Fill a glass with crushed ice and add the sugar syrup, vodka and mint leaves. Mix really well and then top up with enough grapefruit juice to fill the glass. Mix briefly.

Garnish with the sprig of mint and lemon wedge.

Serves 1

# Rumble in the Jungle

50ml dark rum
15ml lime juice
25ml clementine juice
10ml sugar syrup
Ice, for shaking and serving
100ml ginger beer

**TO SERVE**
Crystallised ginger
Dash of Angostura bitters
Twist of orange rind

Add the rum, lime juice, clementine juice and sugar syrup into a cocktail shaker, fill with ice and shake really well to combine.

Strain into a tall glass, fill with ice and pour in the ginger beer. Garnish with the crystallised ginger, add a dash of Angostura bitters and finish with a twist of orange rind.

# Pink Responsibly

40ml pink grapefruit gin
10ml lychee liqueur
5ml maraschino
15ml pink grapefruit juice
15ml lemon juice
15ml strawberry cordial
2 dashes cherry bitters
Ice, for shaking and serving
100ml grapefruit soda
Candy floss, to garnish (optional)

Pour all of the ingredients, except the soda and candy floss, into a cocktail shaker, fill with ice and shake really well to combine.

Strain into a tall glass, fill with ice and top up with the soda. Garnish with the candy floss, if you like.

# Jalisco Sunset

40ml tequila
20ml Aperol
20ml lime juice
15ml agave syrup
Ice, for shaking and serving

**TO SERVE**
Twist of orange rind
Edible flowers

Pour the tequila, Aperol, lime juice and agave syrup into a shaker, fill with ice and shake really well to combine.

Strain into a glass and fill with ice. Garnish with a twist of orange rind and edible flowers.

# Limoncello & Basil Spritz

50ml limoncello
15ml lemon juice
5ml sugar syrup
10 basil leaves, plus a sprig to serve
Ice, for shaking and serving
75ml prosecco
25ml soda water
Twist of lemon rind, to serve

Add the limoncello, lemon juice, sugar syrup and basil leaves to a shaker, fill with ice and shake really well.

Strain into a wine glass and then top up with the prosecco and soda water.

Fill the glass up with ice and then add the basil sprig and lemon rind to serve.

*Serves 1*

# Watermelon Daiquiri

15ml sugar syrup
15ml lime syrup
50ml watermelon purée
60ml white rum
Ice, for shaking
Watermelon wedge, to serve

Add all of the liquid ingredients to a cocktail shaker and fill with ice, then shake really well.

Strain into a coupe glass and garnish with a watermelon wedge.

*Serves 4*

# Pink Maple Lemonade

100ml maple syrup
30ml framboise (raspberry syrup)
300ml lemon juice
250ml water
Ice, to serve
Raspberries, to serve

Mix all of the ingredients, except the raspberries, together in a pitcher and chill for 1 hour.

Fill glasses with ice and pour in the lemonade. Garnish with raspberries.

# Elvis Milkshake

2 scoops vanilla ice cream
2 tbsp peanut butter
1 banana, peeled
200ml whole milk

Add all of the ingredients to a blender and whizz until completely smooth.

Pour into a glass to serve.

Serves 1

# The Big Breakfast Smoothie

75g frozen strawberries
1 banana, peeled
30g porridge oats, plus extra to serve
1 tbsp runny honey, plus extra to serve
2 tbsp natural yogurt
200ml whole milk

Add all of the ingredients to a blender and whizz until smooth.

Pour into a glass and top with a pinch more oats and a drizzle of honey to serve.

# Morning Glory

75g frozen papaya
75g frozen mango
75g frozen pineapple
1 passion fruit, pulp only
300ml apple juice
½ tsp ground turmeric
1 tbsp cashews

Add all of the ingredients into a blender and whizz until completely smooth.

Pour into a glass to serve.

Serves 1

# Blue Monday Smoothie

75g frozen strawberries
75g frozen blueberries
350ml apple juice

Add all of the ingredients into a blender and whizz until completely smooth.

Pour into a glass to serve.

# Green is Good Smoothie

75g frozen mango
A large handful baby spinach
6 mint leaves
350ml apple juice

Tip all of the ingredients into a blender and whizz until super smooth and thick.

Pour into a glass to serve.

To mention even one name would open the door to the impossible. So we won't. Ali and I have surrounded ourselves with so many good people over the years, it's our one and only superpower. Good hearts, hard work, a wicked sense of humour and all-round loveliness are the cornerstone of so many of the people we have worked with. We have been very, very lucky. A huge thank you to everyone who has come on this ride with us, who helped us down some wonderful paths and who helped us back again when we took a wrong turn.

To the millions of lovely faces that have entrusted us with their most important meal of the day, we salute you. You made all this possible. Thank you for giving us a chance.

To our families who deal with the endless uncertainty of this industry and the highs and lows that are part and parcel of every day. Thank you for your support and patience.

Actually, I will name someone. I was the one who got to write this, so there's a chance some of this might be misinterpreted as taking credit. So just to make sure we're 100 per cent clear, I'd like to thank my best friend and sister-in-law for being the best 'bidness' partner ever. You put the heart and soul into this business and everybody who follows, follows in your footsteps. Well done Ali, we did good. (Yeeeek!)

# INDEX

## A

aioli, herb 90, 128
all American, the 42
American cheese slices
    beer cheese 122
    cheese sauce 122
    grilled cheese 79
    Philly cheese patty melt 94
    pulled pork sandwich 96
    The Breakfast Club Burger 70
Aperol
    breakfast negroni 144, **145**
    jalisco sunset 148
apple, blueberry overnight oats 105
apple juice
    blue Monday smoothie 152
    green is good smoothie 152
    morning glory 151
Applewood smoked Cheddar cheese
    bacon, avocado & Applewood sandwich 66, **69**
    posh sausage sandwich 67
aubergine, Turkish eggs 23
avocado
    bacon, avocado & Applewood sandwich 66, **69**
    bean shakshuka 20
    breakfast burrito 83
    Club Med Benedict 29
    egg & cheese 71
    huevos rancheros 18
    smashed avo & pico de gallo toast **114**, 115

## B

bacon
    the all American 42
    avocado & Applewood sandwich 66, **69**
    the big stack 44
    the chocolate & bacon bananaganza **48**, 49
    eggs Benedict 24
    the full Monty **58**, 59
    the greasy spoon 57
    pancakes & bacon 39
    the perfect bacon roll 64, **65**
    The Breakfast Club Burger 70
    The Breakfast Club club 90
bacon lardons, Jonnie's mac & cheese 89
banana
    banana bread 108
    banana bread with roasted peaches 109
    the chocolate & bacon bananaganza **48**, 49
    Elvis milkshake 149
    Guilt-Free Banana Split **112**, 113
    The Big Breakfast smoothie 151
BBQ sauce 121
bean(s)
    bean shakshuka 20, **21**
    chipotle & tomato sauce 129
    the greasy spoon 57
    huevos rancheros 18
    see also Breakfast Club beans, The
beef see salt beef; steak
beer cheese 122
    pulled pork beer cheese Benedict 30, **31**
beer pulled pork 121
    pulled pork beer cheese Benedict 30, **31**
    pulled pork sandwich 96
berries
    Pancakes, Cream & Berries **40**, 41
    see also blueberry; raspberry; strawberry
big stack, the 44, **45**
black bean
    chipotle & tomato sauce 129
    huevos rancheros 18
black pudding, the full Monty 59
bloody Mary
    bloody Mary batch mix 139
    Greek bloody Mary 140, **141**
    Ruby Murray Mary 140, **141**
    The Breakfast Club bloody Mary 139, **141**
blueberry
    blue Monday smoothie 152
    Guilt-Free Banana Split 113
    Pancakes, Cream & Berries **40**, 41
    see also blueberry compote
blueberry compote 135
    blueberry cheesecake pancakes 51, **52**
    blueberry cream 132, **133**
    blueberry overnight oats 105, **106**
bread
    The Breakfast Club club 90
    see also breakfast rolls; brioche; brioche buns; ciabatta rolls; English muffins; sourdough
breakfast burrito 83
Breakfast Club beans, The 120
    bean shakshuka 20, **21**
    the full Monty 59
    veggie spoon 61
Breakfast Club bloody Mary, The 139, **141**
Breakfast Club club, The 90, **91**
breakfast rolls
    the perfect bacon roll 64, **65**
    posh sausage sandwich 67
brioche, crunchy nut French toast **98**, 99
brioche buns
    avo, egg & cheese 71
    bacon, avocado & Applewood sandwich 66
    The Breakfast Club Burger 70
bubble & squeak
    salt beef 62
    sweet potato, Savoy cabbage 63
burgers
    Philly cheese patty melt 94, **95**
    The Breakfast Club Burger 70
burnt chilli butter **22**, 23
burnt onion cream 74, 126
burrito, breakfast 83
butter, burnt chilli **22**, 23
buttermilk fried chicken 34, 86, **87**

## C

cabbage
    sweet potato, Savoy cabbage bubble & squeak 63
    see also pickled red cabbage

caramel sauce/syrup
   the chocolate & bacon bananaganza 49
   salted caramel & chocolate sauce 135
caramelised onions 126
   the big stack 44
   chorizo & Cheddar sausage rolls 73
   Philly cheese patty melt 94
   salt beef hash 97
Cheddar cheese
   bacon, avocado & Applewood sandwich 66, **69**
   beer cheese 122
   breakfast burrito 83
   chorizo & Cheddar sausage rolls **72**, 73
   grilled cheese 79
   Philly cheese patty melt 94
   posh sausage sandwich 67
   pulled pork sandwich 96
   salt beef bubble & squeak 62
cheese
   avo, egg & cheese 71
   Club Med Benedict 29
   grilled cheese 79
   Jonnie's mac & cheese **88**, 89
   Philly cheese patty melt 94, **95**
   posh sausage sandwich 67
   pulled pork sandwich 96
   Reuben sandwich 93
   *see also* American cheese slices; beer cheese; Cheddar cheese; cheese sauce; cream cheese; mozzarella; Parmesan cheese; red Leicester cheese
cheese sauce 122
   the big stack 44
   chicken Kiev sandwich 74
   Nashville fried chicken 34
cheesecake cream 134
   blueberry cheesecake pancakes 51, **52**
cherry compote 135
   cherry cream 132, **133**
   cherry pie pancakes 50
chicken
   breakfast burrito 83
   buttermilk fried chicken 34, 86, **87**
   chicken Kiev sandwich 74, **75**
   cornflake crusted fire wings 84
   fried chicken escalopes 85
   Nashville fried chicken 34

The Breakfast Club club 90
chilli butter, burnt **22**, 23
chimichurri 127
   disco fries 80
   steak & eggs 17
chipotle
   chipotle & harissa mayo 71, 128
   chipotle & tomato sauce 18, 129
chips, ham, egg & chips Benedict 32, **33**
chocolate
   the chocolate & bacon bananaganza **48**, 49
   chocolate cream **133**, 134
   Mississippi mud pie pancakes 47
   salted caramel & chocolate sauce 49, 135
chorizo
   breakfast burrito 83
   chorizo & Cheddar sausage rolls **72**, 73
   eggs al Benny 28
   huevos rancheros 18
   *see also* vegan chorizo
ciabatta rolls, chicken Kiev sandwich 74
cinnamon
   banana bread 108
   maple porridge 105
Club Med Benedict 29
coconut flakes (toasted)
   banana bread with roasted peaches 109
   breakfast sundae 110
   Guilt-Free Banana Split 113
   pineapple & lime overnight oats 105
compotes *see* blueberry compote; cherry compote
coriander (fresh)
   bean shakshuka 20
   chimichurri 127
   chipotle & tomato sauce 129
   disco fries 80
   huevos rancheros 18
   pico de gallo 127
   Turkish eggs 23
cornflakes
   cornflake crusted fire wings 84
   Jonnie's mac & cheese 89
   *see also* crunchy nut French toast
cream
   cheesecake cream 134
   cherry cream 132, **133**
   Jonnie's mac & cheese 89

lemon cream 132, **133**
Mississippi mud pie pancakes 47
passion fruit cheesecake cream 134
salted caramel & chocolate sauce 135
*see also* burnt onion cream; vanilla cream
cream cheese
   cheesecake cream 134
   passion fruit cheesecake cream 134
crunchy nut French toast **98**, 99
cucumber
   dill pickles 131
   Greek bloody Mary 140, **141**

# D

daiquiri, watermelon 149
dill pickles 131
disco fries 80, **81**
drinks 137–52

# E

egg(s) 11–35
   avo, egg & cheese 71
   banana bread 108
   chorizo & Cheddar sausage rolls 73
   classic pancakes 39
   cornflake crusted fire wings 84
   fried 13
      the all American 42
      the big stack 44
      chicken escalopes 85
      disco fries 80
      the full Monty 59
      the greasy spoon 57
      ham so eggcited 43
      huevos rancheros 18
      salt beef bubble & squeak 62
      salt beef hash 97
      steak & eggs 17
      sweet potato, Savoy cabbage bubble & squeak 63
      The Breakfast Club Burger 70
      veggie spoon 61
   fried green tomatoes 123
   hollandaise 130
   homemade hash browns 82
   poached 13
      bean shakshuka 20
      Club Med Benedict 29
      eggs al Benny 28

eggs Benedict 24, **25**
grand royale 26
ham, egg & chips Benedict 32, **33**
Nashville fried chicken 34
pulled pork beer cheese Benedict 30, **31**
rise & shine 57
salt beef bubble & squeak 62
steak & truffle Benedict 35
sweet potato, Savoy cabbage bubble & squeak 63
Turkish eggs **22**, 23
posh eggs on toast 16
scrambled 13
vanilla French toast mix 134
Elvis milkshake 149
English muffins
   Club Med Benedict 29
   eggs al Benny 28
   eggs Benedict 24
   grand royale 26
   ham, egg & chips Benedict 32
   Nashville fried chicken 34
   pulled pork beer cheese Benedict 30, **31**
   steak & truffle Benedict 35
escalopes, fried chicken 85

# F

French toast *see* vanilla French toast mix
fries, disco 80, **81**
full Monty, the **58**, 59

# G

gammon steak, ham, egg & chips Benedict 32, **33**
gin
   breakfast negroni 144, **145**
   pink responsibly **146**, 147
ginger beer, rumble in the jungle **146**, 147
glazes
   honey mustard 43
   Nashville 34
grand royale 26, **27**
granola
   banana bread with roasted peaches 109
   breakfast sundae 110

Mississippi mud pie pancakes 47
grapefruit juice
   breakfast mai tai **142**, 143
   morning mojito 144, **145**
   pink responsibly **146**, 147
greasy spoon, the 57
Greek bloody Mary 140, **141**
grilled cheese 79

# H

halloumi, Club Med Benedict 29
ham
   ham, egg & chips Benedict 32, **33**
   ham so eggcited 43
hash browns 82
   bacon, avocado & Applewood sandwich 66
   the big stack 44
   the full Monty **58**, 59
   the greasy spoon 57
herb aioli 90, 128
hollandaise 130
   Club Med Benedict 29
   eggs al Benny 28
   eggs Benedict 24
   grand royale 26
   ham, egg & chips Benedict 32
   steak & truffle Benedict 35
homestyle potatoes 124, **125**
   the all American 42
   the full Monty 59
   salt beef hash 97
   veggie spoon 61
honey mustard glaze 43
huevos rancheros 18, **19**

# J

jalapeño
   bacon, avocado & Applewood sandwich 66
   breakfast burrito 83
   disco fries 80
   huevos rancheros 18
jalisco sunset 148
Jonnie's mac & cheese **88**, 89

# L

leek
   Jonnie's mac & cheese 89

salt beef 120
lemon
   bloody Mary batch mix 139
   blueberry compote 135
   blueberry overnight oats 105
   cherry compote 135
   lemon cream 132, **133**
   lemon meringue pancakes 46
   pink maple lemonade 149
lime & pineapple overnight oats 105, **106**
limocello & basil spritz 148
lychee liqueur, pink responsibly 147

# M

mac & cheese, Jonnie's **88**, 89
mai tai, breakfast **142**, 143
mango
   green is good smoothie 152, **153**
   morning glory **150**, 151
maple syrup
   maple porridge 105, **107**
   pink maple lemonade 149
maraschino, pink responsibly **146**, 147
marmalade margarita **142**, 143
Martini Rosso, breakfast negroni 144, **145**
mayo
   chipotle & harissa mayo 71, 128
   herb aioli 90, 128
   Virgin Mary mayo 66, 128
meringue, lemon meringue pancakes 46
milkshake, Elvis 149
mimosa, rise & shine **142**, 143
Mississippi mud pie pancakes 47
mojito, morning 144, **145**
mojo picón 127
   disco fries 80
   smashed avo & pico de gallo toast 115
morning glory **150**, 151
morning mojito 144, **145**
mozzarella
   grilled cheese 79
   Jonnie's mac & cheese 89
   pulled pork sandwich 96
mushroom
   the full Monty **58**, 59
   rise & shine 57
   veggie spoon **60**, 61

mustard
    BBQ sauce 121
    bloody Mary batch mix 139
    honey mustard glaze 43
    Philly cheese patty melt 94
    Reuben sandwich 93
    salt beef bubble & squeak 62
    scrambled tofu 119

# N

Nashville fried chicken 34
Nashville glaze 34
negroni, breakfast 144, **145**

# O

onion *see* burnt onion cream; caramelised onions; pink pickled onions
orange juice
    bloody Mary batch mix 139
    rise & shine mimosa **142**, 143

# P

pancakes 37–51
    the all American 42
    the big stack 44, **45**
    blueberry cheesecake pancakes 51, **52**
    cherry pie pancakes 50, **53**
    the chocolate & bacon bananaganza **48**, 49
    classic pancakes 29, 39, **40**, 41–51, **45**, **48**, **52–3**, 97
    ham so eggcited 43
    lemon meringue pancakes 46
    Mississippi mud pie pancakes 47
    pancakes & bacon 39
    Pancakes, Cream & Berries **40**, 41
panko breadcrumbs
    fried chicken escalopes 85
    fried green tomatoes 123
    Jonnie's mac & cheese 89
    mojo picón 127
papaya, morning glory 151
Parmesan cheese
    cheese sauce 122
    ham, egg & chips Benedict 32
    Jonnie's mac & cheese 89
    posh eggs on toast 16

passata
    Greek bloody Mary 140, **141**
    The Breakfast Club beans 120
passion fruit
    breakfast sundae 110
    Guilt-Free Banana Split 113
    morning glory 151
    *see also* passion fruit cheesecake cream
passion fruit cheesecake cream 134
    passion fruit cheesecake waffle 100, **101**
pasta, Jonnie's mac & cheese **88**, 89
peaches, banana bread with roasted peaches 109
peanut butter, Elvis milkshake 149
pepper (green), Philly cheese patty melt 94
pepper (red)
    eggs al Benny 28
    pico de gallo 127
pepper (roasted)
    bean shakshuka 20
    chipotle & tomato sauce 129
    mojo picón 127
Philly cheese patty melt 94, **95**
pickled red cabbage 126
    cornflake crusted fire wings 84
    disco fries 80
    salt beef hash 97
pickles
    dill pickles 131
    *see also* pickled red cabbage; pink pickled onions
pico de gallo 127
    breakfast burrito 83
    cornflake crusted fire wings 84
    huevos rancheros 18
    rise & shine 57
    smashed avo & pico de gallo toast **114**, 115
pineapple
    breakfast mai tai 143
    ham so eggcited 43
    Guilt-Free Banana Split 113
    morning glory 151
    pineapple & lime overnight oats 105, **106**
pink maple lemonade 149
pink pickled onions 126
    avo, egg & cheese 71
    bacon, avocado & Applewood sandwich 66

cornflake crusted fire wings 84
disco fries 80
salt beef hash 97
pink responsibly **146**, 147
pork *see* beer pulled pork
pork sausage
    the all American 42
    chorizo & Cheddar sausage rolls **72**, 73
    the greasy spoon 57
    *see also* chorizo
porridge oat(s)
    the big breakfast smoothie 151
    blueberry overnight oats 105, **106**
    classic pancakes 39
    maple porridge 105, **107**
    pineapple & lime overnight oats 105, **106**
potato
    ham, egg & chips Benedict 32, **33**
    ham so eggcited 43
    homemade hash browns 82
    salt beef bubble & squeak 62
    sweet potato, Savoy cabbage bubble & squeak 63
    *see also* homestyle potatoes
Prosecco
    limoncello & basil spritz 148
    rise & shine mimosa 143
puff pastry (ready-rolled), chorizo & Cheddar sausage rolls **72**, 73

# R

raspberry
    Guilt-Free Banana Split 113
    Pancakes, Cream & Berries **40**, 41
    passion fruit cheesecake waffle 100
red Leicester cheese
    cheese sauce 122
    grilled cheese 79
    huevos rancheros 18
    Jonnie's mac & cheese 89
    pulled pork sandwich 96
Reuben sandwich **92**, 93
Reuben sauce 128
rise & shine 57
rise & shine mimosa **142**, 143
rocket
    grand royale 26
    steak & truffle Benedict 35
rose harissa
    chipotle & harissa mayo 71, 128

disco fries 80
Nashville fried chicken 34
The Breakfast Club beans 120
vegan chorizo 119
Ruby Murray Mary 140, **141**
rum
    breakfast mai tai 143
    rumble in the jungle 147
    watermelon daiquiri 149
rumble in the jungle **146**, 147

# S

salmon, smoked, grand royale 26
salt beef 120
    Reuben sandwich 93
    salt beef bubble & squeak 62
    salt beef hash 97
salted caramel & chocolate sauce 49, 135
sandwiches
    bacon, avocado & Applewood sandwich 66, **69**
    chicken Kiev sandwich 74, **75**
    grilled cheese 79
    posh sausage sandwich 67, **68**
    pulled pork sandwich 96
    Reuben sandwich **92**, 93
    The Breakfast Club club 90, **91**
sauces
    BBQ sauce 121
    chipotle & tomato sauce 18, 129
    Reuben sauce 128
    salted caramel & chocolate sauce 49, 135
    wing sauce 84, 131
    *see also* cheese sauce
sausage
    the big stack 44
    chorizo & Cheddar sausage rolls **72**, 73
    the full Monty 59
    posh sausage sandwich 67, **68**
    The Breakfast Club Burger 70
    *see also* pork sausage
shakshuka, bean 20, **21**
smoothies
    the big breakfast smoothie **150**, 151
    blue Monday smoothie 152, **153**
    green is good 152, **153**
sourdough
    grilled cheese 79
    Philly cheese patty melt 94
    pulled pork sandwich 96
    Reuben sandwich 93
    *see also* toast (sourdough)
spinach
    chicken Kiev sandwich 74
    green is good smoothie 152
    veggie spoon 61
spritz, limocello & basil 148
steak
    steak & eggs 17
    steak & truffle Benedict 35
strawberry
    the big breakfast smoothie 151
    blue Monday smoothie 152, **153**
    Pancakes, Cream & Berries **40**, 41
sundae, breakfast 110, **111**
sweet potato, Savoy cabbage bubble & squeak 63

# T

The Breakfast Club Burger 70
tequila
    jalisco sunset 148
    marmalade margarita **142**, 143
toast (sourdough)
    bean shakshuka 20
    the full Monty 59
    posh eggs on toast 16
    smashed avo & pico de gallo toast **114**, 115
    steak & eggs 17
    Turkish eggs **22**, 23
    *see also* vanilla French toast mix
tofu, scrambled **118**, 119
tomato
    bloody Mary batch mix 139
    chipotle & tomato sauce 18, 129
    fried green tomatoes 90, 123
    the full Monty **58**, 59
    pico de gallo 127
    rise & shine 57
    Ruby Murray Mary 140
    veggie spoon 61
    *see also* passata
tomato (sun-dried)
    avo, egg & cheese 71
    Club Med Benedict 29
    vegan chorizo 119
tortilla wraps
    breakfast burrito 83
    huevos rancheros 18
triple sec
    breakfast mai tai **142**, 143
    marmalade margarita **142**, 143
truffle paste/purée
    posh eggs on toast 16
    steak & truffle Benedict 35
Turkish eggs **22**, 23

# V

vanilla cream 132, **133**
    blueberry cream 132, **133**
    cherry cream 132, **133**
    cherry pie pancakes 50
    the chocolate & bacon bananaganza 49
    chocolate cream **133**, 134
    lemon meringue pancakes 46
    Mississippi mud pie pancakes 47
    Pancakes, Cream & Berries **40**, 41
vanilla French toast mix 134
    classic French toast 99
    crunchy nut French toast **98**, 99
vegan chorizo **118**, 119
    rise & shine 57
veggie spoon **60**, 61
Virgin Mary mayo 66, 128
vodka
    Greek bloody Mary 140
    morning mojito 144
    Ruby Murray Mary 140
    The Breakfast Club bloody Mary 139

# W

waffle, passion fruit cheesecake 100, **101**
watermelon daiquiri 149
wing sauce 48, 131

# Y

yogurt
    banana bread with roasted peaches 109
    the big breakfast smoothie 151
    blueberry overnight oats 105
    breakfast sundae 110
    Guilt-Free Banana Split 113
    pineapple & lime overnight oats 105
    Ruby Murray Mary 140, **141**
    Turkish eggs 23

**EBURY PRESS**

UK | USA | Canada | Ireland | Australia
India | New Zealand | South Africa

Ebury Press is part of the Penguin Random House group of companies whose addresses can be found at global.penguinrandomhouse.com

Penguin Random House UK
One Embassy Gardens, 8 Viaduct Gardens,
London SW11 7BW

penguin.co.uk
global.penguinrandomhouse.com

First published by Ebury Press in 2025
1

Copyright © The Breakfast Club 2025
Photography © Lucy Richards 2025

The moral right of the author has been asserted.

Penguin Random House values and supports copyright. Copyright fuels creativity, encourages diverse voices, promotes freedom of expression and supports a vibrant culture. Thank you for purchasing an authorised edition of this book and for respecting intellectual property laws by not reproducing, scanning or distributing any part of it by any means without permission. You are supporting authors and enabling Penguin Random House to continue to publish books for everyone. No part of this book may be used or reproduced in any manner for the purpose of training artificial intelligence technologies or systems. In accordance with Article 4(3) of the DSM Directive 2019/790, Penguin Random House expressly reserves this work from the text and data mining exception.

Writer: Jonathan Arana-Morton
Publishing Director: Elizabeth Bond
Recipe Writers: Matt Goussaert
   & Scramble LDN
Designer: Studio 7.15
Photographer: Lucy Richards
Production Controller: Percie Bridgwater

Colour origination by Altaimage Ltd
Printed and bound in Germany by Mohn Media GmbH

The authorised representative in the EEA is Penguin Random House Ireland, Morrison Chambers, 32 Nassau Street,
Dublin D02 YH68.

A CIP catalogue record for this book is available from the British Library
ISBN 9781529960112

Penguin Random House is committed to a sustainable future for our business, our readers and our planet. This book is made from Forest Stewardship Council® certified paper.